MONEY MANUAL

Bernard A. Borgnis

ISBN: 147016065X
ISBN 13: 9781470160654

Dedication

This manual is dedicated to the many people who always seem to be living on the edge of not quite having enough money and having just enough money.

TABLE OF CONTENTS

INTRODUCTION

I CREATED THIS MANUAL AS A GUIDE to money and its management as it relates to the pursuit of Freedom, by way of budgeting household income and expenses during one's working life. It is my financial philosophy—a perspective of and about money I have developed over the course of my life. It is my belief that you may benefit from my point of view about the care and purpose of money.

This is not a book of revelations about the management of household income. It is not filled with secrets about how to manage money (because none exist) but with common knowledge that is not recognized by many people. I envisioned this book more as an awakening of your conscious mind to the knowledge of your subconscious mind about the management of money.

To manage money it is necessary to be actively and continuously aware of what you do with your money. There is a need to always know how money comes into your possession and how it leaves your possession and to analyze the two acts to make the best use of your money.

ENOUGH

HOW MUCH INCOME IS ENOUGH? Some do not have enough. Others have more than enough. And still others never have enough. A million dollars would allow you to live a rather extravagant and excessive lifestyle. Foolishness! Many millions would allow you to live wastefully and ridiculously. Embarrassing and absurd!

The correct answer is the amount that enables you to live reasonably comfortably.

Enough to pay all your bills on time each month and every month, giving you stress-free peace of mind.

Enough to go out for lunch or dinner every week or so at a moderately priced restaurant (more often would be wasteful) and perhaps a more expensive restaurant on a special occasion such as a birthday, anniversary, graduation, or retirement to make the event exceptional.

Enough to go away for the weekend once or twice a year. Everyone needs to get away now and then.

Enough for a nice family vacation or stay-cation once a year as well, to build memorable moments in the life of a family.

Enough to be involved in a hobby or two. Participating in personal interests and being creative are very mentally gratifying and rewarding.

Enough to be able to be involved in a club or organization for simple satisfying self-interest.

Enough to be able to own a nice house, free and clear, by the time you retire, if that is your desire.

Enough to help your kids pay for their education so that when they graduate they will not have to begin their life deep in debt. Doing this is as beneficial for the parents as it is for the son or daughter. You will feel good about yourself and happiness for them. They would start from zero, a fair place, instead of from minus, an unfair place.

Enough to enjoy a comfortable retirement, ideally with the love of your life.

I believe all of the above is possible.

Know the importance of money and of how hard it is to come by without being obsessed by it. Life is filled with cycles. When times are good and you have more than enough money, do not think or take for granted that you will always have enough. Remember when you did not have enough and know those lean times will come around again. Save and plan for their return. The surest way to financial Freedom and a secure retirement is a plan of slow and constant saving and investing. Over a lifetime, it will provide you with quite enough.

CARE & RESPECT

MANY PEOPLE ARE GOOD AT EARNING MONEY; even more are good at spending money. The key is learning how to manage money in order to save enough of it. The less you earn, the more crucial it is to manage it better. Those that make more than enough can afford to splurge a bit, buy a few "toys," spoil themselves. Those who make a lot of money will waste much of it.

There is no such thing as a baseball card or a painting or any other item worth tens of thousands or hundreds of thousands or millions of dollars. From time to time, we hear about these kinds of prices being paid. Simply because someone is willing to pay an outrageous amount of money for something does not mean it is worth an outrageous amount of money.

"There's a sucker born every minute" is a quote by David Hannum that is mistakenly attributed to P.T. Barnum. * It is truth.

Investing is cool, fun, and exciting, at least when the stock market and the balances on your statements are going up. When they go down it may not be as cool or as much fun, but it is still exciting. Taking a cruise is fun exciting. A roller coaster is scary exciting. Both are great experiences if you learn to accept and enjoy the ride, knowing in the end you will be on solid ground.

Talking about the stock market and whether it is going up or down and why it is doing either is almost as popular a topic of discussion as sports. Many of us grow up playing

---

* Brown, R.J.,"P.T. Barnum Never Did Say 'There's a Sucker Born Every Minute,'" http://www.historybuff.com/library/refbarnum.html

sports so we have an interest in and a basic knowledge and understanding of them enabling us to talk confidently about them.

Most of us also have a reason and should have at least some interest in the stock market. Retirement income will depend on it, whether you invest knowingly through an IRA or 401(k) or unknowingly through an employer-sponsored pension plan.

Budgeting is considered boring by many people. Because we grow up participating in games and sports, we understand competition and, for the most part, enjoy it. Viewing the budget process as a competition will make it—if not enjoyable—less boring. Making a budget for the year is like making a game plan. At the start you know what you need to do to be successful. The opposition will try to disrupt your game plan. In football there are turnovers, loss of yardage, blocked kicks and punts, and first down denials.

In budgeting there are unexpected expenses such as home and auto repairs or medical bills. The challenge is to be able to deal with and overcome whatever setbacks occur. Be prepared by making a budget and compete against yourself to meet that budget. When you do, you will feel good about yourself for having won the budget game.

Start by developing an interest in and respect for money itself. Coin collecting as a hobby, is an enjoyable way to do this. Finding the coins yourself with maybe a little help from friends and family who know of your interest and putting them into a coin book teaches you to always be on the lookout for money. Coin collecting as an investment, involving the purchasing of coins is not as enjoyable and teaches nothing.

Every time you get out of the car in a parking lot, look around on the ground for coins that others have dropped. This will help you develop the habit, by keeping at the forefront of your mind, the search and rescue of money. This in turn will instill in you the awareness of money-saving opportunities.

To add more interest to found money, check the date. Where were you that year? What did you do that year, or did anything of significance happen to you? Did something historical happen that year?

When I was twenty years old, I traveled with my uncle in the carnival. He was always walking around and looking down at the ground. I asked him why, and he explained, "People sometimes lose money and it falls to the ground. You would be surprised at how much I find." He had a large coin collection.

Coins get no respect, especially pennies. People will not bend over and pick them up. They lose them in cushions, leave them in drawers, and throw them in fountains. People simply do not seem to care about coins, but pennies are money, too, and they add up to dollars.

I see people take money out of their pocket, wallet, or purse and it is facing every which way, crumpled, and mangled. This shows no respect for money at all, and I cringe at the site. If you can disrespect your money, can you not also disrespect property and people, including yourself? How is it that you can treat something that you have worked hard for and that can do so much for you like crumpled trash?

You take care of your house and your car because you worked hard for them and want them to last a long time. You worked hard for the money that bought those things, so take care of it and it will last a long time as well.

Un-crumple, face, and stack your money neatly with all the corners flat before putting it in your wallet. Show some respect!

Learning to guard against the waste of money should become as instinctive as the awareness of safety. It is instinctive to be safety conscious when using a knife, scissors, saw, hammer, or lawn mower, or when looking both ways before crossing the street. Learning to guard against the waste of money should become instinctive as well. Take care of your money and it will take care of you.

STAGES OF LIFE

THERE ARE FOUR STAGES OF LIFE. Little lessons learned and small steps taken to save money over the first three Stages of life will reap the reward of financial security and Freedom in Stage Four.

STAGE ONE of life is for education and training. Education ends when you finish secondary school. Training in a chosen field is most beneficial to earn a living. I've heard people say, "Find what it is you love to do and make that your career." It sounds like good advice, but it is not necessarily so. What if what you love to do doesn't pay well? How happy will you be and for how long if while doing what you love, you are also struggling to make ends meet? Chose a career that you don't mind doing or that you enjoy in a field that pays enough to support the way you want to live. You'll be happier longer.

Vocational training and apprenticeships that teach a trade or craft are excellent ways to acquire skills with which to earn a living, especially for those who like working with their hands, building, constructing, and fixing things. Plumbing, electrical, HVAC technician, and carpentry and its related crafts (such as sheet rocking, roofing and flooring, siding, cabinet making, tiling, landscaping, and masonry) are all trades that will always be in demand.

Roughly a million new households are established every year. Houses are being built every day somewhere, and they will all require maintenance and repair.

Automobile mechanic, paint and body technician, machinist, toolmaker, heavy equipment operator, tractor-trailer driver, cook or chef, and many more occupations require training that isn't all academic. There are a lot of cars on the road and they will require repair and maintenance. Trucks transport everything, and they need drivers and mechanics. People like to eat out, so restaurants need cooks.

For those who prefer occupations that require four or more years at a college, you have great choices, such as lawyer, doctor, scientist, nurse, technician, teacher, journalist, accountant, or any type of engineer.

The reason and purpose for going to college should be seen as a way to get training in a field in which you intend to earn your living.

At the end of Stage One, you should be trained in something that will earn you a living that will satisfy you. If at the end of Stage One you have no training and no skills, join the majority and just find a job. Life will just be a lot tougher.

STAGE TWO of life is the shortest. Some skip it, not realizing its importance. Others refuse to mature and never let it end. Stage Two is the year or two— or maybe even three—after you have finished school and before you decide to settle down and get serious about your life. They are short and sweet yet very important years in a life. Enjoy being carefree for awhile.

STAGE THREE of life is the long row we all hoe. These are the years in which you acquire experience through the trials, tribulations, and triumphs of your life. It is the thirty to forty year period that begins after Stage Two or, for some, after Stage One. Schooling is over and training is finished. It's time to go to work.

During these three or four decades you may decide to marry and raise a family. You may decide to buy a house.

These are options. What you must do and shall do is earn, save, and invest money. These are not options: they are essential in your quest for financial security. How you handle your finances during this third part of life will have a profound affect on your forth part of life, when rest and relaxation are deserved.

We work to earn money, but there are different categories of workers. There are those who love their work, cannot wait to get to work, and basically "live to work." Their work becomes their life, and it seems to define them. Looking at this group, I recognize, though fail to understand, their need to work all the time. Are they workaholics? Is this an addiction or merely a devotion? Without their work they don't know what to do with themselves. Their work gives their life purpose. As I see it, the more hours spent at work, the fewer hours spent at home with family and the fewer hours spent living.

I once worked with a guy who, when he became eligible to retire, said, "If I retire what am I going to do when I get up in the morning?" He was not alone in thinking that way.

What of the group of people who work all the time because of greed? They will never have enough money. Their favorite pastime is watching the balance on their account statements rise. They are hoarders of money.

Then there is the group of people who work more than they would like, not for the love of the work but strictly for the money to meet bill payments and reach the goals they have set for themselves. A lower skill level earns less money and therefore requires more work hours. This group of people "work to live." The work is okay, and it has to be done. These are people doing important work that a lot of other people don't want to do, like the jobs on the television shows *Dirty Jobs* (Discovery Channel) or *Undercover Boss* (CBS).

These workers find employment they do not mind doing. They want to put in forty hours and go home. If they work more, they want the overtime pay. They are there to make money to live a chosen lifestyle and reach the financial goals they have set for themselves. Their love for life and their enjoyment of life come from what they do outside of work.

It is important to understand that workers are important for production and to provide services. Consumers are needed to purchase those products and services. Workers and consumers are one and the same people and are equally important for the economy to properly function.

During Stage Three of life you will budget to save money. Spending money is easy; anybody can do it. Saving is difficult because of the discipline required to control your wants and to not spend unwisely. Managing the money you earn is essential, and the use of a budget is the only way to manage your income. It will minimize the amount of money you lose track of and maximize the amount you have to save. Budgeting will show where adjustments can be made to match "money in" with "money out."

You will also invest during Stage Three for two reasons: first, to keep pace with inflation. Inflation acts as an invisible thief of your money. Second, you will invest to increase the amount of your savings. You will not reach your goals without the help you get from investing. Saving alone is not enough.

STAGE FOUR of life is retirement. Retirement is the time when you can relax and enjoy the rewards of your labor. It is a time in your life when you can replace the rigidity of a schedule with the flexibility of a routine, feel free to come and go as you please, and perhaps even try something new just for fun. The point is that after the thirty to forty years or more of your working life, you want to retire with plenty of life yet to live.

Some people reach retirement age and do not want to retire. Good for them. Those that reach retirement age and cannot afford to retire are the ones I feel bad for. Poor money choices or habits in part three of life will delay part four. Since no one knows how long they will live, extending part three of life and delaying, thus shortening, part four is sad.

My father did not live to retirement; he died at age fifty-four. My grandfather filed for Social Security benefits at age sixty-five and a month or so before his actual retirement date. One day during that time period he came home from work, got out of the car, sat on the ground, and said he "didn't feel right." He died of leukemia eight months later. They were hard-working men who never got the chance to relax and reflect on their lives. Do not work or put yourself in a situation where you have to work until your last days on earth.

When you do retire, you do not want to have thoughts of, "If only I had..." or "I should have..." or "Why didn't I..." Instead you want to cherish the memories of your life that began as dreams. Be proud of the way in which you lived your life. Be pleased with what you have done and not disappointed in what you have not done. And with financial security, continue on your journey through a life of Freedom.

FREEDOM

THE STATUE OF LIBERTY, to me, is the representative symbol of Freedom. On my dresser I have a Danbury Mint* statue of the Statue of Liberty. Every morning, as I take my socks from the top drawer, I look at it and appreciate the Freedom I have and the Freedom it represents. On my left arm is a tattoo of the Statue of Liberty (see cover), signifying Freedom's importance to me.

In school we learned that Christopher Columbus discovered America and that the Pilgrims landed at Plymouth Rock. People have been coming here ever since, seeking a new beginning or an opportunity for a better life. They came as "subjects" of a kingdom and were ruled by a king whose authority was derived from heritage.

The United States of America was founded by people who fought a revolution in order to create a country of Free and independent "citizens" who are governed by a written Constitution and a representative government.

Freedom is the ability to make your own choices about the way you want to live your life: to live as you choose and where you choose; to live and let live; to believe what you will and allow others to do the same; and to come and go as you please. Do not impose your beliefs on others or permit their beliefs to be imposed on you.

In the world today, revolutions are taking place because people want Freedom. Freedom must be fought for; it is never granted. Wars are fought to gain Freedom or to remain Free.

---

* The Danbury Mint is a marketer of collectables.

Dictators who come to power by force and rule by intimidation are on the decline. *Let Freedom Ring.*

Personal Freedom must be achieved as well. It takes many years, and it occurs when your desire for accumulating material things is gone, when all that you ought to do has been done and when you learn that living a life Free from financial worry is genuine Freedom.

True individual Freedom cannot exist without economic security and independence —Franklin Delano Roosevelt.

PLAN

Planning is bringing the future into the present so that you can do something about it now. * —Alan Lakein

SETTING GOALS IN OUR LIVES and for our lives is a good thing. Goals give our lives reason and purpose. Each person can set goals that he or she would like to pursue and, with discipline and perseverance, achieve. Goals can be many and varied. For instance, you may start with the goal to learn to play a musical instrument or speak a foreign language, or to buy a car or take a trip to a place you have heard or read about, or to climb a mountain or take a cruise. Many people share the goal of home ownership. There is no limit to the goals you can choose to set for yourself. The setting of a goal is easy but having the discipline, persistence, and patience to accomplish those goals is not easy.

Unhappiness with your current financial situation and a desire to improve your monetary lot in life are motivating factors in setting a goal for financial security. To begin the process, just set the goal.

Every January people set goals for themselves. Most do not reach those goals. You might be one of them. You may have decided to join a gym to get in shape or to quit smoking. Whatever the goal was, you made a commitment to yourself to put in the effort necessary to achieve that goal. After a few days, weeks, or maybe even a month or more, something happened. The discipline disappeared and with it went the

---

* Alan Lakein, *How To Get Control of Your Time and Life* (New York: Peter H. Wyden, Inc., 1973)22

ability to persevere. Eventually you realized that achieving the goal was not as easy as it sounded inside your head when you first thought of it. You surrendered, thinking you just do not have what it takes to reach that particular goal.

You are wrong. You took the first step and set the goal. Many people never do. They live their lives day by day and paycheck to paycheck and will worry about tomorrow when it gets here. Having a "live for today" philosophy may be satisfying for some, but planning for tomorrow is wise for all. You will want to be able to look back with pride at what you have done in your life and how you lived it. Set realistic and achievable goals. No fantasies allowed.

Where you came from is not as important as how you live your life or where you end up. If you came from a bad environment, were underprivileged, or were not very well off, you do not have to end up there. You can set goals for yourself that will improve your life. How you start out in life is not an acceptable excuse for where you finish. Instead, use it as motivation to improve your situation. To start out poor, work hard all your life, and end up no better off would be a shame. It does not have to be that way.

What is needed to accomplish a goal is a plan. If you set a goal for yourself, it is vital to have a plan to achieve that goal. Wanting to achieve is not a plan. Wishing to achieve is not a plan. Hoping to achieve is not a plan. Want, hope, and wish all express a desire for something to occur without doing anything to cause it to occur. Praying could help; you would actually be doing something. A plan is a course of action, a method by which a goal can be achieved. Freedom is the ultimate goal.

The writers of the Declaration of Independence were very wise men. They put into words our *self-evident truths* and our *unalienable rights,* of *Life, Liberty, and the pursuit of Happiness.* Notice the order in which those words appear: a Life of Liberty brings Happiness.

The First Amendment of the Constitution of the United States guarantees certain freedoms: those of religion, of speech, and of the press. There is no guarantee of financial Freedom. The goal of financial Freedom and a secure retirement is one I believe should be pursued by all. You have to achieve financial security for yourself by yourself. With it, you will know Freedom.

The degree and depth of happiness and success you achieve in life will be limited by those on whom you rely. Be independent and self-reliant, take care of yourself and your family, and you cannot be disappointed. Relying on others can and will lead to disappointment. A willingness to work and strive for the goals you have set will result in success and happiness.

A plan for financial security cannot be implemented without adequate finances. You earn money from the work you do, but work is not a goal. It is the tool we use to achieve our goal of financial security—of Freedom.

Look at the alphabet. A is the beginning of your life. Z is the end. You want to get to R (retirement) with a lot of life left before Z. The goal of being retired with financial security never changes. The methods used to get there do not change but are always improving. The plan, or course of action, is continuously adjusting to life's events.

Formulate your life plan in your mind. Think about it from time to time. Allow it to be flexible. Recognize that it must and should be flexible. Events will occur during your pursuit of financial security that will require flexibility in the plan. Remember that to retire with financial security—Freedom—is your destination.

When I was twelve years old, I made plans with a friend. We would take a cross-country trip on Harley-Davidson motorcycles when we were twenty-one. I do not know what became of that friend because we lost touch, as happens with childhood friends. Age twenty-one came and went as well, but in my mind the trip always remained. In 1980, at age twenty-six, I took that trip of Freedom and adventure. It capped my Stage Two of life, and then I was ready to move on to Stage Three.

The plan was to take Interstate 80 across the country, the most direct route, but allow for flexibility. I gave myself permission to make side trips along the way to discover and experience new and different things or, as on one such side trip, to repair a broken gearshift lever. After taking a side trip, I would always make my way back to I-80 because I knew it was the best route to my destination. Flexibility is very important in any plan.

So let's now map out a plan for financial Freedom.

START HERE

YOU WILL BEGIN YOUR JOURNEY on the road to financial security with money earned, which enables you to function and participate in society. There are also the required acts of conserving dollars while expanding their use in representing the income portion of the household budget.

PAYCHECK Your primary source of income will be your paycheck, and the typical household in the twenty-first century requires two.

It is fine and wonderful if you have young children and it is financially possible for one parent to stay home. Not paying for child care saves money. Over a thirty-year working lifetime, however, it is a poor choice to have only one paycheck contributing to a household's income. At some point in time the decision must be made for the stay-at-home parent to return to work.

The advantage of having two paychecks coming into the household, even if they both are not necessary to cover budgeted expenses, is twofold: saving for college educations and saving for retirement. The amount of money that would be brought into the household by the stay at home parent, compounded over a twenty year period or even a ten year period, is too large a sum to disregard.

It is generally accepted that retirement begins when you are eligible for Social Security, but retirement should begin when you can afford it. Two incomes contributing toward the goal of early retirement for both people makes it more probable you reach your goal on time. Being able to retire at age fifty-nine and a half, the age at which penalty- free withdrawals can be made from an IRA or 401(k) account, is optimal.

Gross pay is the amount of our paycheck you would like to have control over. In actuality the government takes a portion of your money; first with income taxes, to *provide for the common defense* and *promote the general welfare,* then with payroll taxes for Social Security and Medicare to assist us in old age. Fine reasons all. Health insurance premiums are also deducted, as well as pension payments, should you be fortunate enough to have an employer that provides one. There will most likely be deductions for 401(k) contributions, which provide you with retirement income. There may also be additional optional deductions such as an HSA (Health Savings Account) or a Flexible Spending Account (FSA) for health care and/or child care. You will have to balance your household budget on what is left, which is your net pay. Your pay stub may resemble the following:

Pay Stub

Gross Pay	Not Enough
Federal Income Tax	Too Much
State Income Tax	Too Much
F.I.C.A. (Social Security)	6.2%
Medicare	1.45%
Retirement	Future Benefit
Health Insurance	Current Benefit
401k	Match to 5%
F.S.A./H.S.A. Health	Great Idea
F.S.A. Child Care	Very Good Idea
Union Dues	If Applicable
Net Pay	Not Enough

WORK RELATED NOTE: A thirty-minute ride to work is reasonable and acceptable. Any amount over that should be added to work hours. Let us say you earn $15 an hour, work forty hours per week, and drive thirty minutes to get to work. You earn $600 a week ($15 per hour times forty hours equals $600). If your drive to work is sixty minutes, you earn $13.33 per hour ($600 per week divided by forty-five hours equals $13.333333 per hour). The extra half hour drive to work each way adds an hour to your workday for which you are not paid. It should also be added to your workweek hours because it cannot be added to your personal life hours. The same holds true for salaried employees. Include excessive commute time into your hours worked to figure your hourly pay. Know what your time is worth.

Remember, time is money.—Benjamin Franklin.

> The average annual money income before taxes per household is $62,481, of which wages and salary are $49,568. After tax income is $60,712. Personal taxes are $1,769; the difference between $62,481 and $60,712. Source: Bureau of Labor Statistics, Consumer Expenditures Survey, Table 2, 2010 (bls.gov).

These government statistics imply the average consumer household has an additional income of $12,913. Many households do not have that additional income. Household income before taxes is $62,481, minus gross wages of $49,568, which equals $12,913 of other source income. Let's break this down.

$49,568 ÷ 52 weeks = $953.23 per week ÷ 40 hours = $23.83 per hour

Include the $12,913 of other source income;

$62,481 ÷ 52 weeks = $1201.56 per week ÷ 40 hours = $30.04 per hour

A lot of people are not earning $23 to $30 an hour, hence the need for two incomes per household just to reach average.

SALES People don't help themselves often enough by waiting for what they want or need to go on sale. They have to have it when they want it since they work hard for their money and so believe they deserve it sooner, not later. Failure to shop wisely, be patient, and wait for a sale causes them to pay more. When it comes to groceries, buy extra when something that you use a lot of is on sale. Plan you meals for the week based on what is on sale that week.

COUPONS Clipping and using coupons to purchase what you need is smart. Many people feel it is not worth their time to save a few cents. Is clipping coupons wasting time or saving money? Using coupons is to your advantage. Not using coupons is to the store or product manufacturer's advantage. They will gladly keep those few cents you cannot be bothered with. Pennies add up to dollars.

An article in *The Wall Street Journal* titled "Doing the Math on Coupons" written by Brett Arends (Feb. 9, 2010) demonstrates with simple math the money-saving capabilities of coupons. For coupon skeptics this is an important read.

STORE/CREDIT CARDS Surprisingly, they can stretch your dollars. A store card for a grocery store gets you store discounts. Have one for each grocery store you shop at. A store credit card, such as a JC Penney or Kohl's credit card, will provide special offers and discounts as well. Limit yourself to just a couple from stores you usually buy things from like clothes. Avoid carrying a balance on them.

WAREHOUSE STORES If you are willing to buy and/or have the need to buy in bulk, stores of this type, like Costco, B.J.'s, and Sam's Club, can save you money. You need the room to store your purchases and to use them often enough to make the cost of the yearly membership they require worthwhile.

WALMART/TARGET The prices here are good, and you do not have to buy in bulk. Prices on many everyday necessities such as soap, shampoo, toothpaste, laundry detergent, and more are meaningfully lower than at other stores. Spend your hard-earned money where you get the most for it.

RESALE SHOPS: Thrift/Consignment/Goodwill Many people have grown up wearing hand-me-downs. Consider the clothes from these stores as other people's hand-me-downs. Children especially outgrow their cloths quickly. Purchasing furniture at thrift stores can also save you quite a bit of money. You can get older quality furniture for much less than brand-new furniture of similar quality and craftsmanship while maintaining your thrift conscious budget—hence the name Thrift.

TAG & ESTATE SALES "One man's trash is another man's treasure" is a familiar saying. A satisfying way to spend a Saturday morning is to go to tag and estate sales. For a fraction of the cost and every bit as good as new, you can buy hand tools, yard and garden tools, and even kitchen tools and pots and pans. Occasionally you may find a good piece of furniture. Every few years have a tag sale of your own to get rid of things you no longer have a use for. Going to yard sales is fun, like treasure hunting. Take the kids and teach them the value of money: go to the store and show them the price of a hammer, then go to a tag sale, find a hammer at a fraction of the new item's cost, and explain to them that the used one can drive a nail just as easily as the new one.

EBAY An online auction is another way to sell things you no longer want. It is more work than a tag sale but equally as effective, especially for selling smaller, easily packaged items.

DO IT YOURSELF (DIY) "I'll figure it out" is a motto of mine, and quite often I do. Learning to do as much of the maintenance and many of the minor repairs around the house as possible will save on service calls and labor charges. Almost everything you can learn to do for yourself will cost about half of what you will pay a "professional" to do it.

Have the self-confidence that you can do it. A good home improvement and repair manual is a good place to start. There are manuals for everything; everything comes with a manual, and many are available online. If you were to go to a vocational school to learn a particular trade, you would receive a book (manual). First you study about how to do the task, then you are shown how to perform the task, and finally you do the task yourself.

Following basic training in the Air Force, I was sent to technical school at Chanute AFB in Illinois to learn and become a certified TIG (tungsten inert gas) welder on jet engines. First we had classroom study with books (manuals), followed by a shop demonstration by the instructor, and finally followed by doing (practicing the particular weld we were learning that day). This is the method by which virtually everything is learned by everyone everywhere.

Culinary school = classroom, demonstration, cook
Teacher = classroom, teachers aid (instruction) to certify, teach
Doctor = classroom, internship, residency, doctor
Drivers license – classroom, road instruction, license to drive

No one is born with know how. The only reason some people know how to do something and others do not is that they used this three-step process to learn to do it. Everyone chooses what they want to learn and then takes these three steps to learn it. They do not know how to do something you do not know how to do because they are smarter than you are but because they chose to learn by way of the three-step process.

As for learning to do things around the house to save money, follow the three steps. Use a manual for your classroom study. I used *This Old House*, a PBS television series, as my instructor/demonstration method. It is the best show for this purpose because they show you how to do where other shows just show you what they do. There is a big difference. Use the Internet to search for free online how to learning, which often includes videos. Finally, go and do it. The more you do the better you get. Do it yourself whenever possible and save money.

Example: the lamp blew out on our rear projection TV, so I called for a repair. They wanted $150 just for the house call plus parts and labor. No thank you. I ordered the lamp online for $190. My wife found a YouTube.com video demonstration on how to replace it, and she and I put it in ourselves in about ten minutes, saving at least the $150 house call.

Use professionals when necessary, but you may be surprised at what you can do yourself.

FRUGAL Be economical, not wasteful with one of your most important limited resources, namely money. Be certain that the money you spend on something could not have been put to better use by saving it. Know that what you buy is worth the amount you are spending. If you spend a dollar on a candy bar that takes one minute to eat, wait ten minutes and ask yourself if you would not rather have kept the dollar. For the minute or so the candy was in your mouth, it did taste good enough to be worth a dollar. Ten minutes later, maybe not.

THRIFT Spend your money in a wise and thought- out manner, not carelessly and without regard to how hard it was to come by. It is something that must be practiced all the time. Too often, people on a two-week pay cycle are rather careless the first weekend they get paid and feel rich. That last two or three days of the second week they are scrounging for enough money to make it to pay day. Sometimes they even end up embarrassing themselves by borrowing from a friend or co-worker. They do not practice thrift. Those who take this temporary borrowing to the extreme are the ones who make payday loans a legitimate business.

$$$

You'll recall that in my youth I traveled with a carnival. I worked in games and was paid 25 percent of gross receipts from the game I worked. The guys who operated the rides were paid salary. They would sign on for the season and be paid weekly. Though it was seasonal work, it was day-to-day living. They were great guys who loved the whole lifestyle of being on the road, traveling town to town, having fun, and being Free. They were unattached to anything or anyone, yet there was a strong camaraderie amongst all the carnies with the show.

There was not, however, much money to be made. The solution to that was to issue each ride jockey a food card along with his or her paycheck every week. Those who were unable to make their pay last the week could get an advance on their next pay. All they had to do was present the card, which had little squares on it with a five or a ten in the square, to the show's owner. They could ask for either a $5 or $10 advance, and with a hole puncher he would punch a hole in the appropriate square. Any advances they received during the week were subtracted from their pay at the end of the week. The few who fell into this habit never did seem to be able to break out of it.

$$$

BOTTLE & CAN REDEMPTION As a kid in the early and mid sixties, we were always looking for empty soda and beer bottles to redeem at two cents apiece. This is still a way to make money. When you look at an empty soda or beer can or bottle, do not see it as trash but as a nickel and redeem it.

ROADBLOCK ONE

EXPENSES ARE LIKE SPEED BUMPS: keep them low and they are manageable. Poor spending habits can do damage, like potholes in the road. To traverse the road to financial security and avoid ending up in a ditch requires the simple creation of a household budget.

A lot of people who are in debt and want to get out of debt do not like the idea of making a budget. They believe a budget will reveal that not just their expenses but also their spending habits do not match their income. Often expenses can be reduced, and they are relieved by that. Poor spending habits must be eliminated, and they are reluctant to do that. They believe a budget will restrict their life. In actuality a budget will Free them.

The budget will show how much money is required each month to live a chosen lifestyle. A budget has two parts: income and expenses. If the money earned does not equal the expenses incurred, changes must be made. You can either increase your income or decrease your expenses. Budgets must match income and expenses dollar for dollar. They must be adjusted each year to accommodate either increases or decreases in either income and/or expenses.

If household income does not match household expenses, there are two options. Option one: increase income by either working more hours or getting a second job. Either of these methods would reduce time away from home and living life.

Option two: decrease expenses by cutting discretionary spending, which is a much easier life adjustment. Then move on to reducing household expenses.

The average annual expenditures per household are $48,109. Some of the most basic include housing: $16,557; utilities: $3,660; food: $6,129, transportation: $7,677; health care: $3,157. Personal insurance and pensions are $5,373.

Source: Bureau of Labor Statistics -Consumer Expenditure Survey, Table 2, 2010 (bls.gov).

These government statistics show the average expenditures per household are $48,109, which is very nearly equal to the average gross wages and salary of $49,568 (see previous section). Hence the importance of frugality.

EXPLANATION: Subtract the $5,373 for personal insurance, pension, and Social Security, and you are left with $44,195 for household income. As you can see, there is a shortfall of $3,914: the difference between $48,109 (average annual expenditures) and $44,195 (gross wages and salary, $49,568) minus personal insurance and pensions.

Note that the basic expenses add up to $37,180, all to be paid for with after tax dollars, which is well below, by $7,015, the $44,195 of after required deductions income, but short by $3,914, the average annual expenditures.

Non-basic household expenditures, such as clothing, entertainment, personal care, gifts, vacation, saving for college, saving for retirement, etcetera can be paid for with the $7,015.

It would appear as though the average household has enough income to cover basic expenses of $37,180 and $7,015 to pay for non-basic spending but is $3,914 short of average annual expenses. Therefore the average household is actually spending $10,929 on non-basic expenditures.

The apparent problem is the mismanagement of household income. It can be surmised that the $3,914 of overspending is in the form of debt accumulation through the misuse and over use of credit cards and home equity.

The following is a sample list of what may be included in a list of a household's budgeted expenses and spending and how to affect each.

RENT/LEASE Control of this expense takes place when choosing where to live before you move in. After you move in, this becomes a fixed expense that you can no longer control. When moving, however, from one rental to another, consider not only the dollar amount of the rent but also what, if anything, may be included in the rent, such as heat and/or electric. Rent may be higher with either or both of these, but the cost of renting may be cheaper in the long run if utilities are included. The landlord does maintenance and repairs—not your money, or time and effort.

MORTGAGE The amount of the mortgage payment is affected by the size of the down payment and the rate of interest. Always get the lowest fixed-rate thirty-year mortgage possible. Ideally it is best to have at least an adequate and acceptable 20 percent down payment. Be sure there are no prepayment penalties. Try to use a community bank or credit union. They are more likely to keep the mortgage in-house. Avoid mortgage companies and large banks. They will most likely sell the mortgage. It is important to have access to face to-face contact with whatever entity holds the mortgage, should a problem arise.

Let's say you buy a house at age thirty and get a thirty-year mortgage. It will be paid for when you are sixty. If you were to sell the house at age forty and buy another one, you would have to get a twenty-year mortgage. Otherwise you won't be able to meet your goal of retiring without a mortgage at age sixty. Know that your house must be paid off by the time you expect to retire; otherwise you can't retire. You don't want and most likely won't be able to afford mortgage payments on the reduced fixed income of retirement.

There was a time when people would celebrate paying off their mortgage. They were right to do so. A mortgage of zero brings great peace of mind and much happiness. It is a proud life accomplishment. Frame and hang a copy on the wall. It is every bit as important as a well-earned and paid for diploma.

HOUSE INSURANCE Insurance companies offer discounts for multiple policies. Insure your house, auto, etcetera with the same company. A higher deductible ($1,000) will also lower your premium payments. The difference between the low deductible/high premium and the high deductible/low premium is money that can be used elsewhere in the budget or saved and invested. Drive safely and defensively.

PROPERTY TAXES When buying a house, take into consideration the property tax rate in the town. The rates are determined by the "mill rate"[1] which varies from town to town.

HOUSE MAINTENANCE Changing the furnace filter and annual servicing prolong the life of the furnace. Draining the water heater once a year can allow it to work more efficiently, as well as help prolong its life. Clean out the gutters in spring and fall. Ever drive by a house and see weeds growing out of the gutter? Never buy that house. Poor outside maintenance

---

[1]   A rate of tax per dollar on the assessed value of a property. One mill equals $0.001.

indicates poor inside maintenance. Spending money on routine maintenance will save money on more costly repairs latter on.

HOUSE REPAIR Houses are called money pits for a good reason. Leaks need to be repaired, whether they are in the roof or a water pipe. Cracks must be fixed, whether in the sidewalk, driveway, or wall. Repairs can be costly. Ignoring or delaying them will cause the house to deteriorate and lose value more rapidly than age alone. Delayed repairs cause worse damage, resulting in even greater repair costs.

GROCERIES Lots of money can be saved here. It's foolish and a waste of money not to use coupons. Buy and plan meals around whatever is on sale, not around what you feel like eating. Greatly limit— if not eliminate— the amount of desserts and snacks you buy. They decrease your health and increase your grocery bill. Buy the food you need before the food you want.

ELECTRICITY Our lives are electric: cell phones, iPods, iPads, laptops, e-readers—all need charging. Appliances are energy-sucking necessities our houses can't operate without. Going green is a nice idea but too costly at the present time. In the future, when it becomes cost effective, it will be a great idea. Until then energy efficiency and conservation will save the most money. A budget plan from the utility company can make a household budget easier to manage. At Christmas it is nice to decorate, but all those lights cost money to operate. Keep an eye on the kilowatt-hours you use each month so you can limit them.

SEWER & WATER Where they are available, city sewer and water are preferable to septic systems and wells. They are treated and maintained by the city, so you don't have to deal with the problems that will occur with septic and well systems. These charges are often included with the property taxes. If you have a septic system, it will need cleaning at your expense.

HEAT/AIR CONDITIONING A good programmable thermostat can save money. Be as warm or as cool as you can afford to be. Natural gas is great for cooking and heating. Oil is expensive and has too unstable a price. If possible use gas and be on a budget plan with the utility company. Payments remain the same, making budgeting easier, like with electricity.

CABLE/SATELLITE There are a lot of great programs and movies on television. The cable and satellite companies have a wide variety of programming packages that offer too many options. TV viewing hours are limited by the responsibilities and obligations of life. Compare the amount of money you are paying each month to the amount of time you are watching TV. Is the value there? Satellite radio is another questionable expense.

PHONE A telephone is a necessity of life. Cell phones can be considered a necessity of life in today's world, if only for the convenience they provide. The question becomes at what price does the convenience become detrimental to the budget? What percentage of calls made each day, the importance of those calls, and the amount of minutes used determine the worth of the phone?

INTERNET The Internet is changing the world in a good way. Having access to it can enhance your life.

CHILD CARE. We love our children very much. They are adorable and a pleasure to have. They must be cared for while we work, and if you do not have a relative who will do it for free or cheap, the cost of outside-the-family child care is steep. Take advantage of a Flexible Spending Account (FSA) for child care, if one is offered by your employer. It helps the budget because pretax money is deducted from your pay into this account. Make your child care plans when you plan your family.

AUTO PAYMENTS Never lease! The cost of a car is not determined by how much you pay for it but by how long you have it and the cost of the repairs you must make to it.

The first time you finance a car, you're excited and happy to have gotten it, and don't mind the payments. It may be financed for four or five years and around about year three, however, you can't wait to get it paid off to rid yourself of those payments.

When you have made your last payment and the car is yours alone, keep it for as long as you can. An eight-year-old car is fairly easy to sell. Automobiles wear out and will need to be replaced throughout your life. Buying a car that is only a year or two old is a very good idea. You can get good quality without the price of new.

Let's say your payments were $300 per month, which was manageable. Now that the car is paid for, you may be tempted to rejoice because the loan burden has been lifted and you now have an extra $300 a month to spend. Continue with the repairs and maintenance on the vehicle because the longer it lasts, the cheaper its cost. Take that $300 and put it into a car fund toward a larger down payment on your next car. Eventually work toward keeping your current car long enough (at least eight years) to be able to save enough to pay cash for your next car. This will save on finance charges.

PERSONAL CARE Haircuts are not cheap anymore. Salons can be expensive when you start adding up cutting, styling, and coloring, but personal care is an expense you can't avoid. Look into the services offered by a hairstyling or barber school, which charge less than professional salons. Many men have very short hair these days, so you can save money by investing in a good set of clippers. If you like a manicure and maybe even a pedicure now and then, know where the money is coming from and save for it in advance.

AUTO INSURANCE By using the same company that carries your homeowner's policy, you will get a multiple policy discount. A higher deductible will lower your insurance premium as well.

It seems like a good idea to have a low deductible because if an accident were to occur, there would be less out-of-pocket cost. Instead, drive safely, thereby diminishing the likelihood of accidents, and opt for a higher deductible ($1,000), which will be moot because of your safe, accident-free driving. A clean traffic record also gets you additional savings through lower premiums.

Where you live will also have an effect on your insurance cost. A town with less traffic congestion may have a lower rate than a town with high traffic congestion.

Safe driving is not enough. There are a lot of aggressive drivers on the road. It is very important to drive defensively and be on the lookout for aggressive, accident-causing drivers.

AUTO MAINTENANCE Routine maintenance such as oil changes, tire rotation and replacement, transmission and power steering fluid, brake replacement, etcetera are all part of normal wear and tear. The cost of these is not included in the cost basis of the car.

AUTO REPAIR When something on the car no longer works, such as a transmission or radiator, it must be repaired or replaced. Find a local mechanic that you can get to know and trust. He can save you money. Too many people overpay for auto repair problems at dealerships and national specialty repair shops. The local guys usually give a better deal.

These repairs are inevitable, so plan for them. These costs must be factored into the cost basis of the vehicle throughout your ownership of it.

GASOLINE As a teenager I could drive into a gas station, buy a dollar's worth of gas, and go cruising. A gas station attendant would pump it into the car. Nowadays, cruising and leisurely Sunday drives, which once upon a time were enjoyed without regard to the price of gasoline, are now budgetary decisions. The driving distance to work is now more of a monetary factor than it ever was.

MEDICAL Health insurance is absolutely helpful, but it doesn't cover all costs. There are premiums (usually deducted from your paycheck), annual deductibles, co-payments, co-insurance, and costs not covered by insurance. It's best to be prepared for these as much as possible. For the most part, medical expenses remain relatively constant year to year. Plan ahead: if you know you will have surgery or a birth next year, save for it in advance.

If you are fortunate enough to work for a company that offers an FSA (Flexible Spending Account) for medical care or HSA (Health Care Savings Account), take advantage of it. They are accounts in which you can have pretax dollars deducted from your pay and put into an account that you will use to pay out-of-pocket medical expenses. (An HRA (Health Reimbursement Account) provides the same tax benefit.) You are prepared for the bills when they come and are saving money on taxes at the same time.

Some employers allow unused funds to be carried over to the next year, but some do not. Carefully estimate your medical expenses for the next year by looking at what they were the previous year. Divide that amount by the number of pay periods in a year to arrive at the amount to deposit into the account each pay day.

If your employer does not offer this type of account, make your own at your bank or credit union and earmark the funds in it for medical purposes. There will be no tax advantages, but you will be prepared.

LIFE INSURANCE Life insurance is an important consideration for anyone with a family, house, and future education costs. Your family will be provided for should you pass away prematurely.

When the "empty nest" years arrive, the house is paid for, and your finances are under control, it is no longer necessary. Spend the premium or save it because life insurance is not the best way to invest for retirement. The benefits to the insurance company exceed the benefits to you. At age eighty-five your policy will most likely terminate because the risk of you dying is too great compared to the payout that will have to be made.

I recommend not purchasing life insurance for children. Instead take the money you would pay out in premiums and apply it to an education fund. There is a far greater likelihood a child will need money to attend college than for a parent to pay a child's funeral expenses.

CHRISTMAS CLUB Christmas is a wonderful time of year, especially for children. It's also the most expensive time of year. As a child you love to receive gifts, and as an adult, giving is more enjoyable. Decide how many people you will give gifts to and the amount you will spend on each. Add it up and divide by the number of pay periods you have in a year. Every pay day, deposit that amount into a Christmas club account at your bank or credit union. When Christmas comes around, you will have enough money for all the gifts on your list, so you won't have to scrounge for money or fall back on credit cards. It is true that you will be paying for Christmas all year 'round either way, but by saving in advance you can earn a little interest. With a credit card, you'll be paying a lot of interest long after Christmas has passed.

VACATION CLUB Taking a vacation or stay-cation every year is a good thing for your life and family. A break in a routine can only be good. The use of a vacation club is as beneficial to your budget as a Christmas club and works the same way. To the best of your ability, decide how much the vacation will cost and, just as described above, divide by the number of pay periods and deposit that amount each pay day into a vacation club. An alternative is to save what your budget allows each pay day and, when vacation time comes around, go or stay where you can afford, even if it's only a picnic in the back yard. The point is to take a break, relax, and enjoy life a little.

NEWSPAPERS/MAGAZINES Newspapers are great. They tell us what happened yesterday and, somehow, at the same time manage to help us stay abreast of current events. Magazines provide the opportunity to focus on a specific area of interest. The number of subscriptions you can afford may be less than the number of interests you have. Be selective.

ENTERTAINMENT/DINING OUT In the day-to-day routine of working, maintaining a home, and raising a family, it is occasionally necessary to take some time to do something you enjoy—something that makes you think, "Moments like this are why I do what I must." Take in a movie, a show, dinner, or anything out of the ordinary that will give you some enjoyment. Plan for it and save for it. If you limit the frequency of these excursions, they will be held in higher regard. Make them routine and they will become ordinary.

CHARITY Choosing to give to a church, charities or organizations or causes you believe in is a personal decision for each of us. No one can afford every donation request made.

GIFTS Births and birthdays, Mother's Day, anniversaries, weddings, showers, funerals —all are occasions for which we give gifts. Give a gift that the recipient either needs or wants to have. Do not give a gift that you want them to have. A donation on behalf of the deceased is appropriate.

CREDIT CARDS The use of credit cards is fine; the misuse is problematic. A great deal of discipline is required in the use of credit cards. Everyone knows it is better to save the money needed to buy something than to charge it. The habit of relying too much on credit cards, like all habits, is easily acquired and difficult to break.

Credit cards are often used to bridge the gap between where we are financially and where we intend to be in a few weeks or months, or maybe next year, or maybe the year after that, especially when we first break away from our parents and discover the price of being independent. Before we know it, we have fallen into the credit card abyss. Early in an adult's working life, this is an understandable problem that many deal with. As time passes income increases and, with a diligent and persistent effort, credit card control is possible. Throughout our lives they'll remain difficult to manage.

Cash-only doesn't always work. A credit card is a useful tool in the management of our lives. When making airline and hotel reservations or when ordering something on line or over the phone, credit cards are a must. They can also be helpful with certain monthly expenses, such as a Netflix or satellite radio subscription, gym membership, or other similar type of regular, routine charges. They can reduce the number of checks written each month. But their use must be closely monitored. When the bill comes in each month, you have to have the money to pay it off to avoid finance charges. Carrying a balance is harmful to the budget.

Sometimes something happens that was not anticipated, and a credit card needs to be used: the car breaks down or the refrigerator stops working. They must be repaired as soon as possible, but without the available funds, the card comes out. Ideally when the bill comes, the money will be available to pay it off. If this is not possible, pay this extra charge off in the fewest number of months possible. A better solution to this problem will be found in the "Victory Lane" section.

Spur-of-the-moment charges are budget killers. You see something and you feel you have to have it now, so you charge it. A new product comes out on the market and you want to be among the first to have it, so you charge it. How silly is it to see people waiting in line for hours to be one of the first to buy the latest and greatest whatever? In this wonderful, innovative world we live in, there will always be another line with the newest, latest, and greatest whatever. If the money will be available when the bill is due, buying it is fine. If the money will not be available, wait until it is before buying. The company isn't going to stop making whatever any time soon.

Credit card companies charge too much interest, have too many fees, and have too high penalties. If you make payments on time, don't exceed your limit, and don't carry a balance, fees are not a problem. But the credit card companies are in business to make money, not to do you a favor. Let their revenue come only from the merchants who accept their cards. Each month when the statement arrives, look not at the balance first but at the finance charge. This should act as a deterrent against unnecessary credit card use. Think about this number the next time you take out your credit card and know you won't have the money to pay it when it comes due. Please wait! If you are paying interest, and sometimes even penalties and fees, every month, realize that with better management of your credit cards, these charges could instead be money you put into savings.

PET CARE Having a pet can enrich your life. They are fun, cute, loveable, and expensive to own. The food and litter (if you have a cat or other indoor-only animal) are obvious expenses, but the shots pets require and veterinary bills can really add up to serious money.

When you take a vacation or even just go away for a weekend, a kennel is not cheap. A two- week vacation could cost $200 before you leave the driveway. All of the costs of pet ownership times the number of pets you have is something to seriously think about before deciding to acquire one. Remember that if you get a dog, walking in all weather and poop scooping is part of the deal too.

COFFEE/SODA/WATER/ALCOHOL/CIGARETTES If it were not illegal, you could save time by putting the money you spend on these in a shredder. Water is virtually free, and the others provide no benefit to your life. If you buy one cup of coffee on the way to work, a soda at lunch, a beer or glass of wine at night, and a pack of cigarettes a day, these few indulgences you feel you deserve could easily total $35per week, $150 or more per month, $1,800 per year or more. This is lost money. Calculate fifty years of this type of spending, but sit down first so you don't fall down when you see the total.

ODDS & ENDS/DEBIT CARDS/POCKET MONEY There always seems to be some little thing or situation you did not think about. You won't be caught wanting or be unable to buy or contribute when you encounter a Little Leaguer selling candy bars or a veteran selling poppies. Maybe it just feels good to put your hand in your pocket and have it not be completely empty. A little pocket money is always nice to have, just in case.

FEES These are charges we can't do anything about and don't pay attention to. They're on the electric, water, phone, TV, and Internet bills. Bank service charges and ATM fees hurt as well. This is where we really get nickel and dime-d as they say.

OTHER Having a large library of CDs, DVDs, video games, and other such things can add up to a lot of money. Money spent on online gaming must also be a concern. Lottery tickets!? The day will come when you think about the amount of money you spent on them and wish you had the cash instead.

A budget includes a list of expenditures and incomes. They may be daily (coffee/cigarettes), weekly (gasoline/groceries), biweekly (paycheck), monthly (electric/phone/etcetera), quarterly (dividends, investment), semiannually (property taxes), or annually (auto taxes), among others. Spent money is gone; it can not be saved for later.

Below is a sample budget, the final destination of net pay. The total in the Income Amount column must equal the combined totals in the Expense and Spending columns. If they do not, start adjusting, start cutting.

Budget

Income			Expense			Spending		
Source	Date	Amount	Payee	Date	Amount	Payee	Date	Amount
			Rent/ Mortgage			Newspaper		
			Groceries			Magazine		
			Electricity			Entertainment		
			Natural Gas/Oil			Charity		
			Phone			Credit Cards		
			TV			Dine Out		
			Internet			Coffee/Etc.		
			Auto Payment			Cigarettes		
			Gasoline			Alcohol		
			Medical Costs			Odds & Ends		
			Family Obligations			Pocket Money		
			Life Insurance			Other		
			Christmas Club					
			Vacation Club					
			Savings					
			Investments					
Total			Total			Total		

By examining the list of household expenses and spending you see that the actual amount of many of these categories is

46¢

not fixed. Choices you make affect the amounts. Many can be limited or reduced, and some can be completely eliminated. All expenses can be reduced. All spending must be limited and/or eliminated. Family Obligations may include child care, child support, or alimony.

NOTE: During the course of a working life, savings and investments are considered expenses and are, equally important as food and shelter. Savings should be viewed as pre-funded future expenses you know are going to occur. Investments are pre-funded retirement income. Plan for both.

$$\$\$\$$$

You may have heard your parents or, more likely, your grandparents talk of the poorhouse. It was described as a place where poor people with no money went to live. As a kid I didn't know whether that was true or not, or if the poorhouse was even a real place. As an adult I learned there was such a place and it exists today in an altered state.

The Poorhouse: America's Forgotten Institution by David Wagner is an exceptional book that explains the origins and progression of the poor in society. Wagner says that the poorhouse was an institution originally conceived as a way to help the poor on a "temporary" basis until they were able to get back on their feet financially. Sometimes this took awhile. The poorhouse was intended "to be a last resort against hunger and homelessness, but not at all a comfortable one."[2]

---

2   David Wagner, *The Poorhouse: America's Forgotten Institution*(Laham,MD: Rowan & Littlefield Publishers, Inc.,2005,49.

The poorhouse may be gone, but not the poor. Today there are homeless shelters and soup kitchens as a "last resort against hunger and homelessness, but not at all a comfortable one."[3] The poorhouse was a place to live, at least for a while. The homeless shelter is a place to stay for the night.

Manage your money so that you never have to relocate to the poorhouse in any manner, regardless of its form.

---

3 Wagner, loc. cit.

ROADBLOCK TWO

NOW THAT EXPENSES AND SPENDING ARE UNDER CONTROL, you come around a curve to find branches have fallen across the road. You must pause to assess and decide how best to proceed. There's no turning back and going around is not an option. The decisions you make to clear the road and how they affect your finances will determine how successful your journey to financial security will be.

WANT can be very expensive. When you buy a car, it will have a basic sticker price, but all the wants (accessories) you add increase that price. If you want a refrigerator with an ice-maker, it will cost more. Having a pet is nice, so you acquire a dog. He is fun and the companionship is great, but he's not enough, you want another. This is a costly decision. Are you happier with two dogs than you would have been with one? Fewer wants are liberating.

BIG is probably not better, but it is more expensive and we like it. It is an attitude really: my big gas-guzzling vehicle is bigger than yours is, therefore I am better than you are. Disregard the bigger payments, vehicle taxes, auto insurance, tire replacement costs, and the like. My house is bigger, therefore nicer than yours is, and so is my yard. That makes me better than you. Even an extra hundred square feet is important in this contest. Pay no attention to the bigger bills for property taxes, homeowner insurance, and repair and maintenance until it comes time to pay for having bigger.

MORE The desire for more is an all too common attitude of many: more clothes, more shoes, more vehicles, more "toys," etcetera. I'm special and I deserve more. I'm better so I should have more. More costs more. No one needs more. Everyone needs enough.

IT'S ONLY It's only a couple of bucks, a few dollars more. Five or $10 is no big deal. These are common viewpoints taken in regard to add-on services for such things as cell phones, cable or satellite television subscriptions, and other things. The big deal is all those smaller dollar amounts can quickly and easily add up to large dollar totals in the budget.

IMAGE Image will bury you in debt for all of your life. It simply costs too much to try to keep up with, stay ahead of, or be like the "Joneses." When you get what they have got, they get something else. Giving up the image you want others to have of you or a falsehood you have of yourself translates into money in the bank. Buy and learn to be content with what you can afford. You will certainly be happier without the debt.

IMPATIENCE Impatience can be costly. If you are not willing to wait before you buy, you will usually pay more than you should. Save money, be patient, and wait to purchase when the price is right and you have the money. When you decide, there is something you would like to buy, determine how long it will take you to save for it based on how much you can afford to put aside each payday toward its purchase.

PRINCIPLES Having a set of principles by which you chooses to live is right and good for most aspects of your life. When it comes to how you spend your money, it can be costly. Refusing to shop at a particular store because you do not like their policies or politics may be in line with your principles but harmful to your wallet. Not everyone can afford to be so principled. It is best not to let your principles interfere with your finances.

SHOPPING/BUYING When making a decision to acquire something, first shop for it. Look for magazine and newspaper articles about the product. Ask friends and relatives if they know of or have opinions on the product. Do online research. Go and look at it. Find out as much as you can about it. This is shopping. Then forget about it.

At some point in time in the future, a day will come and one of two things will happen. Either you will realize you have forgotten about it to the point where you do not care that you do not have it and no longer want it, or you will go and buy it. Your subconscious will make the decision. Your conscious mind can talk your subconscious into anything in a hurry. Given time your subconscious mind can talk your conscious mind out of something you really do not need or want. Give it some time. This will control impulse buying.

SPEND The amount of money you have to spend is equal to the amount you have in checking or savings accounts that is not earmarked for expenses. It has nothing to do with the value of your assets (house) or the amount of credit you can get.

HOURLY COST When you purchase something, register the price of the item in your mind. Divide the price by the amount of your hourly wage from employment. This will tell you how many hours it took you to earn that item. Only you know if it was worth it.

If you are paid salary instead of hourly, this formula still applies. Simply divide your salary by the number of hours you work in an average week to get your hourly wage.

Let us say you earn $12 an hour and buy a $1,200 flat screen TV. It took you one hundred hours to earn that television ($1,200 price divided by $12 per hour wage = working one hundred hours to earn the TV) Keep in mind how many hours you need to work to pay for your groceries, buy an appliance, pay your electric bill, and put gas in your car to go back and forth to work. Perhaps it would be better not to know. Looking at the cost of something in this manner might at least make you pause before purchasing and take the time to think about how to best pay for it.

PRICE & COST The price of anything you buy is how much you pay for it on the day of purchase. The cost of that something is determined by how long you own it, price of repairs made to it (not to be confused with maintenance of it), use derived from it, and the amount you discard it for or sell it for when you no longer want it. Use this formula:

> Purchase price, including finance charges + repairs – selling price = cost divided by how long you had it = worth. Let us say you buy a car (auto payments discussed above touches on this) for $25,000. After five years, you decide to sell it. You did all of the required maintenance on it, including fluids, tires, brakes, and whatever else had to be done. (These maintenance costs are the price you pay for the use you get from the car.) There were never any repairs necessary and the car has 60,000 miles on it. You are able to sell it for

$15,000. In this example, you had no repair costs and got five years of use out of it for $10,000.

Purchase price ($25,000) + repair costs ($0.00) –sale price ($15,000) = $10,000 Did you get $2,000 worth of use per year out of it ($10,000 divided by five years)? Only you can answer that question.

Let us say you keep that same car for ten years and then sell it for $5,000. After eight years however, there was a $3,000 transmission repair.

Using the formula, $25,000 + $3,000 – $5,000 = $23,000 divided by ten years = $2,300.

People who have automotive mechanical skills can obviously save on maintenance and repair costs by doing their own work. This would bring up the possibly acceptable argument that only the cost of parts should be added to the formula and not the labor costs, which could be accepted as also part of the price we pay for the use we get from the car. Calculate it however, you chose; just do not ignore it.

The point is, the longer something lasts, the more you got your money's worth, and this helps stretch your dollars. Having to or wanting to replace things too often is harmful to your finances. Every year that you own something, its cost to you goes down. Eight years of use is good for a car.

CHILDREN Everybody loves kids. Do more children mean more love? Love is not enough. Children also need food, clothing, and shelter. Children ought to be reared, not dragged to adulthood. It is far better to well afford fewer than to adequately afford more.

Whatever your occupation may be, the amount of money you earn is based on that occupation, not on the number of children you have. Based on your household income range as determined by your occupation, and including your spouse, the number of children you can properly afford to have, raise, and help educate is to be seriously considered.

HOME EQUITY LOAN This is a loan taken out against the equity in the home. Anything that is against you is not for you. The equity in your house is an asset. This is the portion of the house that you have already paid for and actually own. The home is used as collateral for the loan. The mortgage is the portion you do not own; the mortgage holder owns this portion of the house.

Homeowners use these types of loans to remodel a house or to build an addition onto a house. They are also used to consolidate credit card debt and to help pay for a child's education. Some people use them to pay for a vacation or to buy a car. These are all foolish reasons to take out a home equity loan and harmful to your financial security.

Remember, the goal is to have no mortgage by the time you are ready to retire so that you can, in fact, retire. Borrowing against the equity in the house greatly restricts your ability to pay off the mortgage before you retire, therefore denying you the ability to retire. You can't be retired and have a mortgage of any kind. Your reduced income won't allow it.

HOME EQUITY LINE OF CREDIT A home equity line of credit is worse than a home equity loan because you spend your home's equity in an ongoing manner as though it were an ATM machine. With a home equity line of credit, you may never pay off your mortgage, therefore preventing you from ever retiring. Never spend your assets.

REFINANCE If you bought a house with a mortgage rate that at the time was the lowest available but higher than current rates, consider refinancing in order to lower your monthly payments. The new lower rate must be low enough to offset all closing costs for the refinancing transaction. Do not refinance to take money (cash as equity) out of your house. This would be equivalent to a home equity loan or second mortgage, which we know to be detrimental to the goal of owning a house free and clear.

INFLATION Like a magician, inflation will make your money disappear right before your very eyes. Inflation is the rate at which the price of things you buy, both goods and services, increases and the purchasing capability of your dollars decreases.

For planning purposes, use 3 percent as the average annual inflation rate. Whatever you bought last year for a dollar will cost you $1.03 this year. Your money is worth 3 percent less this year than it was last year. You would need a 3 percent raise at work just to stay even. The $1,000 you keep under your mattress for emergencies would now really be worth $970 even though you still have the $1,000 there. You do not realize you lost anything because you look and see that the money is still under the mattress. Put the $1,000 in a bank where it will be safe and earn interest and you still lose because the banks are paying less than 1 percent interest. You lose less but you still lose. You would have to find a place to put it where it would earn at least 3 percent to avoid losing buying power.

HOME OWNERSHIP The American dream, or so we have been led to believe, is home ownership. When we own our own house, we feel we have made it. We have succeeded. No landlord or Homeowners' Association with a list of rules to follow—it is our house, and we can do what ever we want to in it. It is the one place where have as much Freedom as the law will ever allow.

At work your boss tells you what to do. The boss has a boss telling him what to do. A CEO has a Board of Directors and shareholders to answer to. Business owners have customers and clients they must please. Everyone has someone telling him or her what to do. In your own house, nobody tells you what to do. You are Free.

SEVEN POINTS ABOUT HOME OWNERSHIP:

POINT ONE: a house should not be considered an investment.

All a house will do for as long as you own it is deteriorate. Everything in it, from plumbing to electrical to roofing and flooring, will in time need repairing, updating, or replacing. Cabinets and appliances last a long time, but eventually they need replacing. Over the course of its life, the maintenance on a house is major and should not be underestimated. The costs associated with this upkeep cannot be disregarded. Because of this, the value of a house that has been well maintained can increase no more than the rate of inflation.

Below is a partial sample amortization schedule for a thirty-year $200,000 mortgage with a 6 percent interest rate. It shows the schedule for one-year and then five-year intervals. Study the columns of Principal Paid, Interest Paid, and Total Interest at each interval.

Amortization Schedule

Year	Month	Payment	Principal	Interest	Total	Balance
2011	March	1199.10	199.10	1000.00	1000.00	199,800.90
	April	1199.10	200.20	999.00	1999.00	199,600.80
	May	1199.10	201.10	998.00	2997.01	199,399.71
	June	1199.10	202.10	997.00	3994.01	199,197.60
	July	1199.10	203.11	995.99	4990.00	198,994.49
	August	1199.10	204.13	994.97	5984.97	198,790.36
	Septembe	1199.10	205.15	993.95	6978.92	198,585.21
	October	1199.10	206.17	992.93	7971.85	198,379.04
	November	1199.10	207.21	991.90	8963.74	198,171.83
	December	1199.10	208.24	990.86	9954.60	197963.59
	January	1199.10	209.28	989.82	10,944.42	197,754.31
(1) 2012	February	1199.10	210.33	988.77	11,939.19	197,543.98
(5) 2016	February	1199.10	267.22	931.88	58,054.78	186,108.71
(10) 2021	February	1199.10	360.44	838.66	111,263.58	167,371.45
(15) 2026	February	1199.10	486.18	712.92	157,935.88	142,097.69
(20) 2031	February	1199.10	655.79	543.31	195,791.42	108,007.17
(25) 2036	February	1199.10	884.56	314.54	221,754.49	62,024.17
(30) 2041	February	1199.10	1193.14	5.97	231,676.38	$0.00

A mortgage of $200,000 indicates a $250,000 purchase price (20 percent down payment of $50,000); add total interest of $231,676.38, and the actual amount paid for the house is $481,676.38. Add original closing costs as well as any costs associated with improvements.

Consider that a $250,000 asset compounded over a thirty-year period at 3 percent (inflation rate) would be worth $606,815.75. The return on investment after thirty years:

Worth ($606,815.75) cost of house ($250,000) interest ($231,676.38) = $125,139.37 –closing costs –upgrades & improvements

In this example, upgrades and improvements over the purchaser's ownership period would have to be less than $125,139.37 to produce a positive return. Many would incorrectly believe their $250,000 "investment" had grown into a $606,815 asset.

With a house paid for in full, at some point in time during retirement you may decide to sell the house and use the money to pay for living expenses. This money should be viewed as money that was saved for retirement. It was saved in a place that paid 3 percent interest on average for thirty years. (Something that is currently very nearly impossible.) It was not money that was invested in the stock market where it would have returned on average 6 percent over the thirty-year period. A $50,000 investment earning 6 percent for thirty years with monthly contributions of $306 would grow to $608,510. The mortgage payments were almost certainly more than $306. For comparison, a $50,000 investment earning 6 percent for thirty years with monthly contributions of $1,199 (the payment amount from the sample amortization schedule above) would grow to $1,505,542.

POINT TWO: some people believe a remodel will increase the value of a house.

This would be true only in the case of a house that has not been taken care of, been allowed to deteriorate, and is sold as a "fix up." The remodel will replace value lost by deterioration through lack of repair and maintenance.

Granite counter tops have become popular. An upgrade from a Formica counter top to one of granite will increase the value of the house by the cost of that upgrade only. Spending $3,000 on a new granite counter top will not increase the value of the house by $6,000.

The exception to this added value rule is an addition to a house. An addition would add value because of the amount of square feet of floor space added to the house. Adding floor space adds value.

It is important to remember to always add the cost of improvements to the cost of the house. It is incorrect to add the cost of improvements to the value of the house but not add them to the cost basis of the house. You fool yourself into believing the equity in the house is greater than it really is and that the house is worth more than it is.

SUMMARY: examples of an upgrade would be increasing electrical service from one hundred amps to two hundred amps or greater or installing a granite counter top or hardwood floors. An example of an improvement would be a room addition, or finishing off a basement because you are adding square feet to the living space.

POINT THREE: the appreciation on a house can roughly be calculated using a 3 percent (the average annual inflation rate) per year rate.

During the real estate boom and before the bursting of that bubble in 2006, many homes were increasing in value by as much as 20 percent and even more in some places with no justifiable reason for such increases. It was not real. A house, like people, spends its entire life deteriorating; its value cannot increase. Upkeep can only allow its value to remain constant, in relative terms, as it relates to inflation.

POINT FOUR: when you decide to sell your house, a real estate agent will usually give you a price range in which they believe, based on their experience, what the house will sell for.

A good agent will give you an honest assessment because it is in their interest to sell the property as quickly as possible. The longer it is on their books, the more it costs them in the way of advertising and time showing the house continuously. When a buyer is found, they apply for a mortgage. Whether it is a bank, mortgage company, credit union, or other entity, they will want to do an appraisal to determine the value of the house. They certainly want to appraise the house for the fair market value in the particular neighborhood based on its condition and what other houses have sold for in the area. An appraisal is subjective. They make money from the interest on the amount of the mortgage. A higher appraisal translates to more money.

Before the real estate bubble burst, lenders were very willing to give buyers mortgages at the high end of the appraised range and even beyond. Everyone was happy. The buyer got the house and maybe a little money back at closing. The seller sold the house for all that they hoped they would, not merely for what they thought they could. The real estate agent received a commission based on a little higher selling price. The lender collected interest on a higher mortgage. The government claimed a higher home ownership rate.

POINT FIVE: each house sold and each time it is sold the price is always higher. (until the real estate bubble occurred).

A deteriorating asset does not increase in value. The seller always wants more money, whether justified or not; he wants all he can get and maybe still just a little more.

This is not to suggest that a seller of a house whose suggested price range is $195,000 to $205,000 and whose house is appraised for $200,000 cannot ask for $215,000 and sell for $210,000. As long as the buyer is qualified, credit worthy, and has a 20 percent down payment, everyone will be happy. Sellers always think their house is worth more than it really is. The seller gets more than the house is worth, so he is happy. The buyer paid less than the asking price so he thinks he made a good deal, and he is happy. The loan provider is happy because he will be earning interest on an extra $10,000. A bit of a gamble on his part but not likely to be a problem as long as he did his due diligence in requiring a 20 percent down payment and made certain of a credit worthy buyer. The housing bubble was caused by not doing due diligence in regard to issuing mortgages to unqualified buyers with no down payments.

POINT SIX: the town you live in re-evaluates your property from time to time, usually every ten years.

They use the same data as the mortgage appraiser. Since the town's revenue comes from tax receipts, it is in their interest for your property to increase in value more than perhaps it should. They were happy when, during the bubble, home values were rising faster and higher than was logical because tax revenue was increasing greatly as well. Homeowners may have complained to coworkers at the time, but did not really seem to mind because they were proud to be able to boast about how much their house was worth. Now that the bubble has burst and home prices are returning to where they should have been, everybody is complaining.

POINT SEVEN: to get a better idea of what the true value of a previously owned house should be worth, visit the Land Records of the house at the Town Hall. Real estate cycles last about eight years on average. It is recognized that real estate prices peaked in 2006 which means the bubble began to inflate in 1998. Go back to that time frame to be certain of being pre-bubble. Use that sales price and a 3 percent per year increase to calculate what the current value ought to be. The next up-cycle in real estate will begin in 2014.

ROADBLOCK THREE

WHILE TRAVELING THE ROAD OF LIFE, you have enjoyed many sunny skies. The occasional thunderstorms you downplayed, however, have created a sinkhole in the road, and the bridge has washed out behind you. You find yourself trapped between your debts. Encouragingly, Freedom can be seen on the distant horizon. The sinkhole of debt can be filled, and the bridge to safety can be rebuilt.

Debt causes first concern, then worry, and, eventually, sleepless nights. If controlled and used in moderation, it can be useful in the pursuit of your goals. The limitless use of debt, however, will never allow you to become financially secure. Debt and financial security are simply not compatible.

CREDIT SCORE Fair Isaac Corporation measures credit risk and assigns a numerical score to it, called FICO score. William R. Fair and Earl Isaac developed the system in 1958. Most people refer to it simply as their credit score. The higher the score, the more creditworthy a person is considered to be.

The benefits of having a high credit score are well known. Good credit allows you to buy things you can't afford to pay cash for. This can be a helpful thing. Since it is not likely you will pay cash to buy a house, a high FICO score would be helpful in allowing you to obtain a mortgage.

Pay all bills on time. Have one general-purpose credit card with zero balance or, at the very least, a balance less than 20 percent, a safe and manageable amount of available credit. More credit cards with balances greater than 20 percent of available credit will hurt your score, and you can get into trouble playing one card off of another. Having good credit is a good thing; having a lot of credit is a dangerous thing.

Too often, however, many use credit for insignificant purposes and even foolish purposes. Knowing that, think on this: the higher the credit score, the more credit you are given. The more credit you are given, the more credit you are likely to use. The more credit used, the more indebted you become. The more indebted you become, the less Free you are.

Credit has the illusion of being an asset, a good thing. It allows you to acquire many things now and pay for them later. This permits the perceived asset of good credit to be in actuality the liability of debt, which is a bad thing.

EXPLANATION: In the case of a credit card with a limit of $10,000, meaning you have a debt allowance of $10,000:

- When you have a $2,000 balance, you have used 20 percent of your debt allowance. You have not used 80 percent of your debt allowance. You are in command of your debt.
- With a $3,000 balance, you have used 30 percent of your debt allowance. You have not used 70 percent of your debt allowance. You are not in command of your debt, but you are still in control of your debt.
- With a $4,000 balance, you have used 40 percent of your debt allowance. You have not used 60 percent of your debt allowance. You are not in command and are losing control of your debt.
- With a $5,000 balance, you have used 50 percent of your debt allowance. You have also not used 50 percent of your debt allowance. You have lost both command and control of your debt.
- With a balance of $6,000 or greater, you have used 60 percent or more of your debt allowance. You have not

used 40 percent or less of your debt allowance. Your debt is now in control and command of you.

Fear of debt is a good thing. If, through poor management of money, you one day realize you are in debt, attack it. Start by eliminating expensive bad habits (smoking, alcohol, gambling). Then reduce all other variable expenses. This money that you are no longer spending must now be applied to your debt in order to eliminate it.

It is necessary to divide debt into two categories: acceptable debt, which we use to accomplish goals that improve our lot in life, such as home ownership and education; and unacceptable debt, which will prevent us from reaching our ultimate goal of financial security and the Freedom it allows.

MORTGAGE DEBT People do not pay cash to purchase a house. Debt in the form of a first mortgage is acceptable debt. Control it by never extending the length of the mortgage. Never take out a second mortgage, home equity loan, or line of credit on a property. Do not buy more house than you can afford. Buy a house that has enough square feet to allow you to live comfortably and without feeling cramped, but not so much space that a lot of it goes unused. You would be paying taxes on, heating, cooling, vacuuming, and dusting space that you do not even use so that you could create an image, and, in the process, you would be turning acceptable mortgage debt into unacceptable mortgage debt.

The objective of the mortgage is to not have one. Never-ending borrowing on the equity in your house is a path to an unhappy Stage Four of life. A mortgage of zero will bring great peace of mind, happiness, pride, and a feeling of accomplishment.

Remember the retirement time frame. When taking out a mortgage, the plan is to pay it off in thirty years or less. To own the house outright and no longer be a part owner with the mortgage holder is the goal.

EDUCATIONAL DEBT Taking on debt for the purpose of education is acceptable debt. It is debt that has value. Though the education can enable you to earn more, the cost of the education may, for some, be prohibitive. The cost of attending some prestigious schools when an equivalent education can be earned at a less expensive school can turn acceptable education debt into unacceptable education debt.

Yearly increases in the cost of education far exceed the rate of inflation. The day is fast approaching, and may have already arrived for some, when the average middle-class family will not be able to afford the cost of higher education. Their son or daughter does not have the grades or a talent worthy of a scholarship. These people will decide that college is just not worth going that far into debt. One day, in the not too distant future, the number of students attending college will begin to decline.

Too many students are graduating with too much educational debt. Student aid in the form of a scholarship or grant is wonderful, if you get it. Student aid in the form of a student loan is a burden.

Colleges need to change their attitudes. Unlike vocational schools, colleges insist students take extra courses (the so-called core curriculum) because they want the student to have what they consider a well-rounded education. In many colleges students take no courses related to their major in their freshman year. The cost of college does not allow for the luxury of taking required yet unnecessary courses in an effort to fulfill the colleges' vision of a well-rounded, educated person. You don't go to college to get a well-rounded education;

you go there to acquire the foundation of your chosen field of study for the purpose of earning a living. If students were not required to take courses unrelated to their major field of study, the cost of college would be significantly reduced and more people could become students.

Should a student wish to enroll in courses of interest outside their main course of study and are willing and able to pay for it, that's fine.

The worth of this debt comes only when the education received leads to financial gain. A good education, whether at a vocational, technical, or academic school, is one in which you learn and train for something that provides you with the ability to earn a good living. Any training or education should be specific to your chosen career field in order to be cost effective. Degrees in medicine, law, teaching, accounting and finance, engineering, and the like are all great.

Specialize! We live in a world of specialization. There are few doctors who become general practitioners. They become specialists. That is where the money is. Learn a skill and become a specialist.

A liberal arts education is a waste of time and money. Look in the want ads of the newspaper. There are jobs for mechanics, machinists, cooks, waitresses, carpenters, electricians, truck drivers, masons, real estate agents, medical technicians, cashiers, laborers, computed-related jobs, accountants, data entry, and all sorts of occupations. There are no ads for liberal arts specialists though. The job that you can get with a liberal arts education you can get without a liberal arts education. Job recruiting websites list jobs requiring specific skill abilities.

Think how ironic it is that a person graduates from college with a liberal arts education —where they are taught by teachers—and can not then get a job as a teacher. Their education had to have been specific to the teaching profession in order to be certified to teach. Why would anyone spend the time and money to earn a degree in nothing in particular?

If the sought after education is merely for one's own desire, self-satisfaction, and enrichment, the cost is too high. Try e-learning at sites like openculture.com. Here you can take courses from many colleges and universities in all kinds of subjects, or simply go to the library. The Internet is a source for many free learning opportunities in virtually any subject or topic at top universities, including Stanford and MIT. Credits are not earned, but a topic is learned. The Khan Academy(www.khanacademy.org) is an excellent not-for-profit online learning site.

Libraries are filled with books that enable people to pursue, on their own, any interest they choose. The same text books used in college classrooms can be bought online. Self-education is easier than ever because of the Internet. Teach yourself these other interests and save money.

Once you have decided, for the right reasons, to take on this debt, it is best to look at it as an investment. On any investment, you want to know where the payoff is. How long will it be before I get my money back and when do I start making a profit? It is not upon graduation, nor is it when the student loans are paid off. Determine the difference between how much you earn with the added education as opposed to how much you would have been earning without it. Divide that number into the cost of your education to arrive at the number of years it will take to recoup the cost of the education. From that point on you are in positive territory realizing gains.

AUTO DEBT Everyone needs a reliable automobile. Auto debt can be acceptable. Control costs by limiting accessories and luxury. Cars deteriorate even more rapidly than houses. Most people can remember the excitement they felt when they first got their driver's license and the. independence it represented. You no longer had to have your parents drive you where you needed to go. Adventure was accessible: you could drive farther than you could walk. Romance was on the horizon: you could date and act cool, even if you were not cool. Cars were distinctive looking: they had style and character. Gas was cheap. Now cars are pretty much clones of one another; not much distinguishes one from the other. Gas is expensive. A car has become, primarily, a utilitarian vehicle.

Do not buy more car than you need. The best way to avoid auto debt is to pay cash. Since this is not always possible, refer to "Auto Payments" in the section "Roadblock One." Buying new is fine, but consider dealer demonstration cars or models left over from the previous year.

MEDICAL DEBT Routine medical expenses such as annual dental and wellness physical exams or any normal medical needs throughout the year should be handled with a combination of health insurance and budgeted expenses. However, the unfortunate development of a serious medical condition may someday occur. Your health is the most important part of life. When your life or the lives of your spouse or children are at risk, medical debt becomes unavoidably acceptable.

There are serious medical conditions that can be prevented or delayed; heart disease is at the top of the list. Half of heart disease is caused by poor diet and lack of exercise; genes and family history affect the other half. To a certain extent, you can control this by developing a lifestyle that includes proper diet and exercise. This is very difficult for many, and perhaps you can slide by in your twenties, but as you pass into your thirties and then your forties, it is imperative that you begin taking better care of yourself with annual check-ups that monitor your current health. If not, you will wish you had by the time you reach your fifties and sixties and you may not want to make it to your seventies and eighties because your physical problems may prevent enjoyment of life. It would be regrettable to wait until it is too late.

I know what I'm talking about because it happened to me. Aging is something you should look forward to, not be afraid of. You want to become a senior citizen in the best possible condition, both physically and financially.

CREDIT CARD DEBT The worst debt of all comes in the form of a little piece of plastic you keep in your wallet. Credit card use is, as stated earlier, fine and often necessary. Credit card abuse, which causes debt, is not fine. You're only fooling yourself if you use credit cards to maintain an otherwise unaffordable lifestyle or to make purchases that project an unfounded yet desired image. The ever-increasing statement balance this causes is unacceptable debt.

Many people do carry a balance on their credit cards, and those balances can get out of control and eventually reach into the thousands and even tens of thousands of dollars. One of the best ways of assuring you will never reach your goal of financial security is to abuse your credit card usage.

Carry only one general-purpose credit card. If your intentions are, as they should be, to pay the full balance when the bill comes due, only one card is necessary. Having more than one card means you know you will be carrying a balance because your budget will not permit paying off all cards every month. It also means you know you can't afford what you are buying.

The best way to avoid credit card debt is to buy only when you know you will have the money to pay for it at the end of the month. Otherwise delay the purchase until you do. The amount of money in your budget that is allocated to credit cards should be equal to the amount you can afford to pay off in full when the bill comes due. Totally disregard the amount the credit card company states is your credit limit. The credit limit amount benefits the credit card company, not the credit card holder. I find it amazing that some people brag about how high their credit card limit is, somehow wrongly thinking this is a good thing. It is a debt trap.

When beginning a debt reduction plan that includes several credit cards, it is highly recommended to pay off the credit card with the highest interest rate first. This saves you interest money. With multiple credit cards, you are paying on each card every month. No doubt they have varying balances. If the balances are all relatively equal, this is the best approach.

An alternative method would be to pay off the one with the lowest balance first, getting rid of it quickly. You can then apply the money you were paying on it in addition to the money you were already paying on the next credit card so that you are paying a greater amount on the second credit card, paying it off quicker. Move to the next card, now making its payment as well as the payment amounts of the other two paid-off cards, making, in essence, a triple payment. This will rid you of credit card debt at an ever-increasing pace. Continue in this manner until all credit cards are paid off. Then keep only one.

Carrying a balance on credit cards and paying the double-digit interest the card companies charge is not a good trade-off for the impatience of buy-now-pay-later. The money paid on a credit card's finance charge is money that could be saved or invested towards a child's education or your own retirement.

Who is Free? The person who possesses nothing and owes no one, or the person who possesses much and owes many?

GAMBLING DEBT This is the most fun debt, and it is unacceptable. Everyone likes gambling because it is exciting. No one likes losing, and as the losses increase, the thrill, hope, and optimism you felt at the start will turn into anguish and despair.

A thoroughly enjoyable way to waste money is casino gambling. The atmosphere in a casino can be exhilarating. The problem is, the odds are always against you and favor the casino. Everyone knows this yet the excitement and the pull of the possibility of maybe winning some money can be irresistible.

Fantasy sports leagues are another entertaining way to lose money as they say, "On any given Sunday." Do not fool yourself. It's all luck. You cannot win anything in which you are not involved and have no effect on the outcome. You are relying completely on others to achieve your goals for you. It makes no sense.

Poker has become so popular that it is now a televised sport. Skill may enable you to stay in the game for a while, but you will lose in the end. Betting money on anything is a long-term losing proposition no matter how often you think you have won in the short term. When on occasion you win, you will feel momentary joy. You feel proud and think you are smart.

When you win, you believe the reason to be that the outcome was a result of 90 percent smarts on your part and 10 percent good luck. When you lose, the reason is your 90 percent smarts lost out to 10 percent of bad luck. You continue to gamble because you know for certain that you always possess the 90 percent smarts. The only gamble is the 10 percent luck factor, which has a 50 percent chance of being either good or bad. Thus you believe the odds are always in your favor because of the advantage you have over others: smarts. You are willing to take the 90 – 50/50 odds every time. They rely on luck. You have smarts.

You will not win your way to your financial goals. Gambling will lead you in the opposite direction. Only having a plan and the discipline to follow it will work.

$$$

Once upon a time, people deep in debt were sent to debtors prison. An excellent book, *Republic of Debt: Bankruptcy in the Age of American Independence* by Bruce H. Mann, is about the evolution of dealing with debtors in America.

Mann writes that before the Revolutionary War, when a person fell deep into debt for whatever reason and was not able to pay his bills, he would meet with his creditor to work out a debt repayment plan, not at all unlike what takes place today in such instances. Then as now, if the debtor continued to not pay, the creditor would sue to get back his money. The difference is that back then, as Mann describes it, "a writ of attachment"... "required the debtor to provide security sufficient to satisfy the debt, using his property if adequate, or his body, if not."* He was imprisoned.

People who become deeply indebted today, though not jailed, are in effect imprisoned by their debt. They are not Free.

$$$

73¢

An indentured servant was a person without funds who would use debt to gain transportation to America and for housing and food after arriving, then work off that debt. Today we still use this system of indentured servitude by making purchases we do not have the money to pay for and then working to pay off that debt.

VICTORY LANE

FOLLOWING THE GUIDELINES OF this manual will bring you successfully to Victory Lane.

In the Beatles song "Can't Buy Me Love," the line "money can't buy me love" is true. Money also cannot buy happiness in the sense that there is not an item, place, trip, or experience whose purchase would translate into happiness, though it can provide enjoyment. Enjoyment is a temporary occurrence. Money can provide happiness by allowing you to live without worrying about paying bills, putting food on the table, or having a place to live. Therefore, though money can't buy happiness, it can provide happiness. Love is not happiness. Two people can be in love, but if they worry about paying bills, they will not be happy.

The connection between saving money and living a happy life is misunderstood. Happy days are lived on the days on which we have all the money we need and want for that day. Money to pay bills due on the day they are due makes for a happy day. No worries. Money to spend on entertainment if that is what we desire on a particular day makes that day a happy day. No disappointment. Money that has been saved and is available on and for all the rest of the days of your life make for a happy life.

In addition to a checking account, there are three types of savings accounts used during the working Stage Three of life. When the need arrives this saved money will solve a problem for you or get you through a financial difficulty. It will help with education and provide for you in retirement.

CHECKING ACCOUNT A checking account is used to receive income and pay household budgeted expenses and other miscellaneous spending on a daily and weekly basis. If you are paid weekly or biweekly, this works very well. If you are paid monthly, half must be kept in the checking account and half in the traditional savings account for use in the second half of the month, at which time you will transfer it back to the checking account.

Checking Account

Purpose	Funding Source	Total
Daily/Weekly/ Monthly expenses and spending	Paycheck	Equal to Daily/ weekly/monthly budgeted expenses

TRADITIONAL SAVINGS ACCOUNT Hold this account at the same bank as your checking account. There is never a lot of money in this account, and its use is primarily to manage money, not to save money. Hold money in excess of what the budget requires near term in this account and any first half monthly deposit of money for use in the second half of month.

Budgeted money for expense items that are due infrequently (quarterly, semi-annually) can be kept in this account until needed.

Traditional Savings Account

Purpose	Funding Source	Total
Infrequent Household Expenses	Checking Account	Monies in excess of budgeted expenses.

IMMEDIATE ACCOUNT The occasion discussed in "Credit Cards" in "Roadblock One" has arrived. A large unexpected auto repair bill has come up or the water heater has stopped working and needs replacing. If there is not enough out-of-pocket money, meaning checkbook and traditional savings account money, to cover the cost, this can be a serious problem. The solution for dealing with these types of problems is the use of an Immediate Account (IA). Put money into this account every payday until the balance reaches at least $3,000. That amount will usually be enough to cover any unforeseen home or auto repair costs. Having this account, is preparing and budgeting for the inevitable unexpected expenses.

Keep this money in a savings account at a bank other than the one that holds your checking account to make it inconvenient, if not difficult to access, reducing temptation to spend it in a way other than its intended use. This is saved money. It does not earn any interest to speak of but is there when you need it quickly.

Homeowners without a mortgage who pay property taxes semi-annually or whose mortgage does not include property taxes should also use this account for that purpose by increasing the amount held in this account to cover those payments. This account will also hold Christmas and Vacation club money to be deposited each payday and withdrawn at the appropriate time.

Immediate Account

Purpose	Deposit Per Pay Period	Total
Large unexpected expenses	What the budget will allow	$3000 to $4000
Christmas Club	Total cost of gifts ÷ number of pay periods	Total cost of planned gift giving
Vacation Club	Cost of vacation ÷ number of pay periods	Cost of planned vacation

EMERGENCY ACCOUNT In the event of sudden job loss, having enough money held readily available in reserve in a credit union or money market account will provide a great deal of relief. The money in this account will provide for living expenses and allow you time to find new employment. Consider this money self-funded unemployment insurance.

This account is also the place to hold the equivalent of both home and auto insurance deductible money. Having a $1,000 auto insurance deductible helps to lower your premiums. If you ever have an auto accident, the money will be readily available here. For the same reason, keep $1,000 to cover you home owners insurance deductible.

As discussed in the "Roadblock One" section titled "Auto Payments" also use this account to hold the equivalent of your car payments after the car has been paid off in order to pay cash for your next vehicle.

These four earmarked monies are kept separate from the rest because they are strictly for emergencies and distant future expenses.

Emergency Account

Purpose	Funding Source	Total
Homeowners insurance deductible	Transfer from Immediate Account	$1000
Auto insurance deductible	Transfer from Immediate Account	$1000
Self-funded unemployment insurance	Transfer from Immediate Account	Equivalent of 3–6 months net pay
Auto Fund	Auto payment equivalent	Projected cost of future auto

HOW TO FUND THE EMERGENCY ACCOUNT (EA) When the amount of money in the Immediate Account (IA) reaches $4,000, take out $1,000 and start an EA. Every time the IA hits $4,000, repeat this transfer until the balance in the EA reaches the equivalent of three months' net pay, plus the equivalent of your insurance deductibles. Those with a less secure job will want to fill the EA with more money perhaps six months' worth of net pay or whatever amount makes you feel secure. The money held in the IA and EA have different purposes, and for that reason it is best to keep them in separate accounts. It simplifies things. This is also saved money. It may earn a small amount of interest if held in a credit union, online savings account or money market account, but its primary purpose is to weather a storm in your life

ALTERNATIVE METHOD—SINGLE SAVINGS ACCOUNT It is not absolutely necessary to maintain different accounts in different banks for different purposes. I find it simpler and less tempting. There is an alternative system requiring a greater deal of discipline: Single Savings account. With this method, simply use a piece of paper to keep track of each type of account, its purpose, the amount contributed each payday, and the total amount required in it.

Single Savings Account

Type	Purpose	Pay Day Deposit	Total Required
Traditional	Infrequent Household Expenses		Monies in excess of budgeted expenses.
Immediate	Large Unexpected Expenses	What the budget will allow.	$3000 - $4000
↓	Christmas Club	Total cost of gifts ÷ number of pay periods.	Total cost of planned gift giving.
↓	Vacation Club	Total cost of vacation ÷ number of pay periods.	Cost of planned vacation.
Emergency	Home-Owners insurance deductible.	Fund with $1000 transfers from IA as they accumulate.	$1000
↓	Auto Insurance Deductible	↓	$1000
↓	Self-funded Unemploy ment insurance.	↓	Equivalent of 3-6 months net pay.
↓	Auto Fund	Auto payment equivalent.	Projected cost of future auto.

The types of investment accounts to be used during retirement, Part Four of life.

401(K) Many employers now provide 401(k) accounts for their employees. This is an investment account for retirement purposes. Contributions grow on a tax-deferred basis. You should absolutely contribute to a 401(k). Some employers match employees' contributions up to a certain percentage of base pay. You should contribute at least up to this match. This matched money is in effect a guaranteed return of 100 percent on contributed investment money.
- You have a choice of what to do with this employer-matched money.
- Choice one: invest it the same way you invest your own contributions, in the stock market where there is risk.
- Choice two: only invest it in very safe government securities to avoid risk. There will still be inflationary risk.
- Choice three: invest the employer match in a dividend-paying stock fund. It will have the growth potential of the stock market and the security of the dividends.

Whether employers match these contributions or not, this invested money will probably provide much of your retirement income. It is imperative to your financial future that you contribute. If an employer-sponsored 401(k) will be your primary source of income in retirement, it becomes vital to contribute. Not contributing will lead to regret in retirement.

It is possible for the money amassed in a fully funded 401(k) to exceed what a standard employer-defined benefit pension plan would provide.

IRA An Individual Retirement Account is used to invest money for retirement. The money put into this type of account is not taxed before entering but is taxed upon exiting. Withdrawals may begin at age fifty-nine and a half and must begin by April 1 of the year after reaching age seventy and a half. When the required minimum distribution time arrives and you find you are not in need of the money, it is permissible to transfer (not tax free) the distribution to a taxable account.

ROTH IRA A Roth IRA is a variation of an IRA and similar to the Roth 401(k), in which contributions are not taxed but withdrawals are. Withdrawals may begin at age fifty-nine and a half. There is no mandatory withdrawal date.

When the amount you contribute to a 401(k) reaches the equivalent percentage of the employer match and you are in a position to contribute more, pause before doing so. Instead contribute additional money to this Roth IRA account. Making after-tax contributions to both a Roth IRA and a Roth 401(k) account may reduce your functioning household income by more than the budget can handle. If that would not be a problem, feel free to do so. Otherwise, have one be a Roth account and the other a non-Roth account.

NOTE: Never borrow from a 401(k) or IRA account. Borrowing imposes a setback in the pursuit of retirement. Loans, even from your own accounts, require you to work longer to reach your goal.

NON-IRA ACCOUNT This is probably my favorite account. It is used to carry you through financially from when you decide to retire to when you begin receiving retirement income, whether it is from Social Security, a pension, IRA, 401(k), or other source.

Choose a mutual fund that invests in dividend-paying stocks. During the course of your investing life, the reinvestment of all dividends and any capital gains is critically necessary. In retirement, have the dividends sent to you for use. Though the value of your shares will fluctuate as the stock market rises and falls, the number of shares you own will never decline as long as you do not sell them. Dividends are paid for each share. The more shares you own, the greater the dividend check you receive.

Particularly in retirement, have money in a dividend-paying mutual fund such as an Equity Income fund. These quarterly dividends will supplement your retirement income. When you retire, gradually transition your other types of mutual funds to dividend-paying funds and interest- paying funds. If you are not in immediate need of the money in your retirement accounts when you retire, leave it there until you do or until you are seventy and a half, when you are required to begin taking at least a minimum retirement distribution. Put those distributions into the non-retirement dividend- paying fund. Buying more shares increases your dividend check. In retirement, dividends are important. Equity Income Funds invest in dividend-paying companies.

NOTE: A No-load mutual fund does not charge a sales commission to purchase shares in the fund before investing your money. A Load fund does charge a commission.

Investment Account for Retirement Purposes

Type	Location	Amount
401k	No-Load mutual fund	Equal to employer match or 5 percent of base pay
Roth IRA	No-Load mutual fund	Same as what would be employer match
Non IRA	No-Load mutual fund	Other available investable money

529 PLAN This is an investment account for your child's future education. Open one account for each child at his or her birth. This allows for eighteen years of contributions and growth of the money. It is a much better method than waiting until the child is a year from high school graduation and then trying to figure out where the money will come from. The money is withdrawn tax-free if it is used for qualified education expenses. State versions are available.

RETIREMENT INCOME

PENSION Working for an employer who provides a pension is obviously beneficial to retirement income. Unfortunately, these are fading away. Pensions are generally 30 percent to 50 percent of the amount you earned during working years. Expenses will not be reduced by an equal percentage at retirement, therefore supplemental income is necessary.

Since the introduction of 401(k) plans in 1982, more and more employers are going that route, making employees' provisions for their own retirement income vital. They should have always felt responsible for supplemental income.

SOCIAL SECURITY An employer contributes 6.2 percent (temporarily lowered to 4.2 percent in 2011,for political reasons, to the detriment of the system's future) of your gross pay to the Social Security Trust Fund. Each employee also contributes 6.2 percent to this fund. Retiring at age sixty-two, the minimum retirement age, will result in a smaller Social Security payment. Delaying retirement until you reach full retirement age results in a larger payment. Retiring sooner means being Free to enjoy life for more years as opposed to retiring later with more money. Which do you value more?

Do not count on this money alone to provide you with all of your retirement income, especially for those under age fifty. You will no doubt get some amount of money from Social Security, but be able to provide for yourself without it. A better plan would call for this money to be pocket money, part of discretionary spending. This will not be enough to live on.

TARGET AMOUNT How much money will you need to retire? This is a question a lot of people ask, and everyone has a different answer.

Consider being average, at least for this exercise. One method of calculating the amount of money you will need at retirement is to use the well-known three-legged stool example: one-third from pension, one-third from Social Security, and one-third from savings/investments.

- Determine the amount of money you will need to live on each year in current dollars.
- Subtract the annual amount you expect to receive from your employer pension.
- Subtract the annual amount you expect to receive from Social Security.
- Determine how many years you expect to live as a retired person.
- Multiply those two figures to arrive at a total.

This is the amount of money you will need to accumulate in your portfolio—the combined total in all of the accounts you intend to use in retirement, such as savings, IRA, 401(k), Roth's, and non-retirement accounts—before you actually retire.

EXAMPLE: If you plan on retiring in 2012, with corresponding numbers above:

- Using Bureau of Labor Statistics(section "Start Here") the average annual household income is $62,481. In retirement, $49,985 (80 percent of $62,481) should be enough because your expenses should be a little lower. If they are not, reduce expenses or keep working. You decide.
- One-third (first leg of the stool) of $49,985 equals $16,662, which is the pension portion of retirement income.
- One-third (second leg of the stool) equals $16,662, which is the Social Security portion of retirement

income. Your annual Social Security printout will show how much you can expect to receive.

- Retiring at age fifty-nine and a half, the earliest age at which penalty-free withdrawals can be made from retirement accounts, and living until age seventy-eight (average life expectancy4*), would allow for eighteen and a half (seventy-eight minus fifty-nine and a half) years of retirement living.

- One-third (third leg of stool) equals $16,662, multiplied by eighteen and a half equals $308,247, the total amount of savings and investment portion of retirement income, to be accumulated prior to retirement for equal distribution during retirement.

This figure represents an approximation using government statistics for average income and life expectancy. If you believe you will live longer, you will obviously need a greater savings and investment portion.

The above example has no meaning to a younger group of people who may not receive a pension and probably do not expect to receive Social Security. It is quite possible all retirement income for them will come from 401(k) and IRA accounts. Therefore, the three-legged stool approach does not apply. This group of future retirees will need a hassock filled with savings and investments.

Using the same government figures would look like this:

Required annual retirement income = $49,985

N/A

N/A

---

* *The World Factbook,* https//www.cia.gov/library/publications

Retired life of eighteen and a half years

Savings/investment total before retiring: $49,985 multiplied by eighteen and a half years equals $924,723 for 2012 retirees.

Using 3 percent inflation rate, $924,723 will need to be $2,244,545 in 2042 dollars.

To reach a total of $2,244,545 would require an investment in the stock market of $3000 to open an account, earning the average annual return of 6% percent and, starting at age twenty-five, monthly contributions to age fifty-nine and a half of $1,613. This can be achieved more easily if both spouses are working and contributing. With an employer match, the household portion of this contribution could be reduced.

The bottom line is that each household must annually examine and recalculate the family financial plan to stay on course to achieve their stated goals.

INVESTING

INVESTING IS HOW SAVED MONEY GROWS. It must grow for several reasons: to keep pace with inflation, which diminishes the value and purchasing power of currently saved money; to pay for the education of children; and to provide income during retirement. Saving alone will not accomplish these objectives.

The fact that you should invest in order to reach the goal of financial security is absolute. As a small individual investor, you should be conservative in your philosophy toward investing. Find a low-cost no-load mutual fund company such as Vanguard Group, T Rowe Price, or Fidelity. Choose from among the index funds and core funds they offer. Invest routinely and consistently for thirty years or more until retirement and beyond.

The first twenty years of a thirty-plus-year investment program is more about share accumulation than account value. Watching the value rise makes you feel good but is not the most important matter during this time. When the market is down, share prices are down, and your money buys more shares. Conversely, when share prices are up, your money buys fewer shares.

When the market drops dramatically, like in a recessionary period or in a "someplace in the world unfortunate event," view this as an occasion to buy more shares with your investment money to build greater wealth for the future and not as a time to despair over lost account value. Do not be concerned with the value of your account if you have more than ten years before you will need the money. Concentrate instead on amassing as many shares as possible. Automatically reinvest all dividends, capital gains, and interest to acquire even more shares.

Those who took advantage of the recent stock market buying opportunities of 2009 and 2011 will, in the years to come, look back on the wisdom of their decisions with great satisfaction.

In the final ten years prior to retirement, begin to concentrate on government securities and bonds and funds that invest in dividend paying stocks. Gradually move to these more conservative types of investments until you reach your target amount needed, especially with new money (see "Victory Lane"). Though this is not a "how to" investment manual, the fact that you must invest to reach your goals has been established; therefore, there are a few things to know:

STOCK MARKET The stock market often retreats but never surrenders. The stock market always wants to go up. Bad news causes it to go down. Fortunately, bad news is always temporary. History shows us that in the long term, things always get better. Over short periods of time, the stock market is a gamble, a loser's game. Invest for the long term and you are sure to win. Over long periods of time, it has always gone up. It is the best place to grow your money at a rate above inflation over a lifelong period.

It is generally accepted that the average annual total return on stock investing has been between 6 percent and 7 percent. This average is a result of a combination of price appreciation and reinvested dividends. Some say it is greater; I prefer to use a more conservative number for planning purposes. Far too many entities that rely on stock market returns have used much higher rates of return projections in their planning, especially during the 1990's, only to find themselves with under funded liabilities later.

Total return includes the reinvesting of all dividends and capital gains. If the market returns are higher, great; but overly optimistic projections often lead to disappointment. Pleasant surprises are far better than disappointing expectations.

COMPOUND INTEREST Like the magic beans that Jack planted, compound interest will cause your money to grow rapidly. At each interest calculation period, whether monthly, quarterly, semiannually or annually, the interest is calculated on the combined principle and interest of the preceding period, as opposed to simple interest where interest is calculated on principle only.

EXAMPLE OF COMPOUND INTEREST: Start with $1000 earning 6 percent interest rate annually for thirty years.

After Year 1, $1,000 × 0.06 = $1,060
Year 2, $1,060.00 × 0.06 = $1,123.60
Year 3, $1,123.60 × 0.06 = $1,191.02
Year 4, $1,191.02 × 0.06 = $1,262.48
Year 5, $1,262.48 × 0.06 = $1,338.23
Year 6, $1,338.23 × 0.06 = $1,418.52
Year 7, $1,418.52 × 0.06 = $1,503.63
Year 8, $1,503.63 × 0.06 = $1,593.85
Year 9, $1,593.85 × 0.06 = $1,689.48
Year 10, $1,689.48 × 0.06 = $1,790.85
Year 15, $2,260.90 × 0.06 = $2,396.56
Year 20, $3,025.60 × 0.06 = $3,207.14
Year 25, $4,048.94 × 0.06 = $4,291.88
Year 30, $5,418.39 × 0.06 = $5,743.49

EXAMPLE OF SIMPLE INTEREST: $1,000 × 0.06 × 30 years = $1,800

In this example, the simple interest gain after thirty years is $800 versus a $4,743.49 gain with compound interest. Obviously compound interest is a beautiful thing. The problem is, at the present time, 6 percent interest is no where to be found.

INVESTMENT EXPENSES Investors often pay too little attention to the cost of investing. Management fees along with a variety of charges and expenses associated with investing hurt investment returns far more than many people realize. Always seek to minimize expenses as much as possible. No-load mutual funds accomplish this.

DOLLAR COST AVERAGING This is the most affordable method of investing. It is the individual investor's method of becoming wealthy enough. At periodic intervals, send money to a mutual fund of choice for investment for future needs. When starting an investment program with limited funds, begin with a payroll deduction of whatever amount you can afford to a credit union account or deposit into a savings account and send it to the mutual fund quarterly or semiannually. In time you may be able to afford to send money on a payday or monthly bases.

NOTE: Do not use dollar cost averaging to purchase individual stocks because the transaction costs involved in doing so would be disastrous to the small amount being invested at any one time.

STOCK INVESTING Stock investing is the buying of a company's stock and gaining financially from price appreciation and/or capital gains and/or dividends.

For an individual to invest in individual stocks is too costly, in both time and money. This must be done through an account at a brokerage company where the fees and commissions are not conducive to money making for small investors with limited funds to invest at any one time. The time, resources, and ability necessary to research stocks is too great. Commissions are paid for each transaction; you pay when you purchase and then you pay again when you sell. Forget this!

The individual investor cannot afford to invest in this manner efficiently. It may be good for your ego and the image you want to project to be able to say, in conversation, "I bought this or that stock" or "I own this or that stock" but it is not good for your wallet. Do not do it!

STOCK TRADING Stock trading is not investing. It is the buying of a company's stock and attempting to gain financially by the manipulation or maneuvering of that stock within the market. I would compare it to playing poker, which is gambling. Do not do it!

MUTUAL FUNDS The ideal way for an individual to invest in the stock market is through mutual funds. Individual investor contributions are pooled together and invested in the stock market by the mutual fund company. This minimizes invest ment risk as compared to individual stock investing because of the funds' ability to diversify among a large group of stocks with the pooled money. Choose a low cost no-load mutual fund company and stick primarily to core and index funds within that company to minimize cost. They will provide enough of a return to meet your financial goals.

CERTIFICATE OF DEPOSIT Eventually, as your portfolio grows, some money can be put into CDs for safety. Invest in these only when interest rates are up—up being at least 4 percent, so as to be above the average inflation rate of 3 percent, and definitely when rates are above 6 percent, the average market return rate. They earn more interest than a savings account and are very safe. The money is illiquid (tied up) for a specific amount of time. When the CD matures, you have the option to reinvest both principle and interest or use the interest to treat yourself. It can be a reward to you for staying on course and sticking with the plan. It is important to reward yourself occasionally. Too often and you would not be rewarding yourself, you would be spoiling yourself, and that is never a good thing. It teaches un-appreciation and entitlement.

GOLD Gold is for making beautiful jewelry and collector coins. It has worked well in recent years as an investment, but over the last one hundred and fifty years, it has not kept pace with inflation. Some view this asset as a safe haven for money.

If you believe, as I do, that gold is being mined every day somewhere and all of it will remain in existence for all of time, and it does not get used up, consequently supply is always increasing. How can its value increase as well? Fear!

Buyers of gold fear losing all the wealth they have. Sellers of gold and those that earn a commission from selling investments in gold convince buyers of gold the sky is falling and they will lose all the wealth they have. They think that if they can get ten people to buy gold and each of them get ten people to buy gold and each of them get ten people to buy gold, and on and on, the price of gold will keep going up and they will all be rich. When the fear is gone, the price will go down.

INVESTMENT PORTFOLIO The group of investments accumulated over the course of a person's investment life is his or her investment portfolio. It may contain the following:

A Roth IRA account, which should not be tapped before age seventy and a half.

A 401(k) account at place of employment.

> **NOTE:** Changing employers allows for the rolling over of the 401(k) into a traditional IRA account. Why do this? First, if you have several employers during your working life and a 401(k) at each, this would allow you to consolidate them into a single account for simplification. Second, the IRA could be at the mutual fund company of your choice, whereas the 401(k) is at the fund company chosen by your employer.

A non-IRA account at a mutual fund investing in dividend-paying stocks and/or interest-paying bonds, or a balanced fund that does both.

Possibly some government bonds, some CDs and of course a savings account and a piggy bank that is full.

RETIREMENT

How beautiful it is to do nothing, and then rest afterwards.
—————————Spanish Proverb

Finally you come to R in the alphabet: Stage Four of life.

If you can get there with a feeling of pride in the way you lived your life and how you treated others, always as equals, never as superior or inferior to ourselves...

If you can get there with regret only for opportunities not taken and not for anything you've ever done...

If you can get there knowing you were always advancing yourself, striving to improve...

If you can get there knowing you have always done the best you could...

If you can get there having done all you were obliged to do and enough of what you desired to do ...

If you can get there with reflections on a life of fulfillment and happiness...

If you can get there with love...you will have accomplished all that is essential here on earth.

Retired. Get a rocking chair. Do something. Do nothing. Go somewhere. Stay home. Read. Watch the grass grow, the flowers bloom, the birds feed; listen to them sing. Or don't. Sit on the porch and watch the world go by. See the clouds passing. Wake up to see the sun rise and then wait to see it set. Watch the leaves bud in spring and fall in autumn. Drive to the ocean and watch the tide advance upon the shore and then retreat. Watch a neighbor mow the lawn. Daydream. Volunteer. Listen to the stories of the elderly. Pursue a hobby. Enjoy not having to do anything. Be Free.

CONCLUSION

BY SPENDING ALL THE MONEY YOU EARN EVERY PAY PERIOD, you very well may live a satisfactory pre-retirement life—quite possibly, even a wonderful life. At retirement, however, when income drops to less than half the amount you were earning, life may be very unsatisfactory. Spending less money than you earn is not enough. It will keep you out of debt, but you will not prosper.

Buying a house may give a feeling of pride. Paying off the mortgage will give a feeling of relief. Freedom.

Quit is the only failure there is. Setbacks in all pursuits are inevitable. Perseverance leads to success. Regret comes from never having tried, not from failure.

A debt collector is the person who accumulates debt, not the person who demands payment.

There is no feeling comparable to having no debt and enough money in the "bank" to not worry.

No amount of money can buy integrity, honesty, morality, loyalty, or dignity; but the person who cultivates these priceless qualities of character is indeed rich enough.

When you decide you want to retire and realize you cannot afford to do so, you will be saddened to look back at how you spent your money throughout the working years of your life and realize how much of it you squandered.

You can have stuff or you can have money, you cannot have both. When you had money, you bought stuff. When you run out of money, you sell your stuff.

Easy Street is one on which many would like to live. If you get there by working hard and living thriftily, you may live there a long time. If in an attempt to get to Easy Street, you rush and borrow your way there, you won't live there very long.

Learn from the experience of this "Great Recession" to spend less and save and invest more in order to be better prepared for the inevitable recessions of the future.

People who believe saving small amounts of money doesn't help have too much money. And those who believe spending small amounts of money doesn't hurt think they have plenty of money.

In the introduction, I said there was not a secret to managing money to attain actual Freedom. There is a way, however, and it doesn't have to be as restrictive as a step-by-step approach. It is quite simply the development of a philosophy that requires a hesitation, a pause, to think and make a conscious decision about the value received of every dollar spent. An understanding that money earned and carefully managed with thrift and frugality incorporated into household finances in order to save and invest can and will provide the Freedom essential to a happy life.

CONCLUSION

If one day you exceed all your expectations and accumulate more than enough money, pay it forward family-style. Help your children and grandchildren. When a good, long, healthy, happy life has been lived and there is money left in the jar, pass it on before you leave. After a lifetime of hard work earning, saving, investing, and enjoying what the money did for you, pass it down and witness what good it can do and happiness it can provide for those to whom you give and love. You experience no enjoyment giving after you are gone.

WHO IS B. A. BORGNIS?

I WOULD DESCRIBE MYSELF AS A MONEY conservationist and Freedom enthusiast. I study the management of money as it relates to the household and its correlation to Freedom.

The oldest of five children of a working-class family my parents divorced when I was eleven. Both parents worked hard at low-wage factory jobs. Financial struggles were the norm.

After the divorce, we still needed two incomes to make ends meet. That meant my mother had to work two jobs, but money was still always in short supply. I wanted to know why. With my awareness and observation of financial struggles, the origin of my view of the relationship between working hard and earning not a lot of money was formulated.

I actually enjoyed hard work. I wanted the hard work to get me somewhere, not something. At age eleven I had my first job. By age fifteen I was working full-time year-round and going to school. Having money gave me a feeling of independence and Freedom. I saved my money, bought myself a car, and felt even greater independence and Freedom. Money made life easier and struggle-Free.

Academics were not my thing. For me, working hard and earning money were easier than studying hard and earning a grade on a report card. I also understood I had no talent from which to profit. I knew I could do two things really well: work hard and save money. They would be my ticket to Freedom.

As I grew through my twenties and learned more about myself, I came to understand that I didn't need a lot of money. I am fortunate to lack the emotion of envy, one of the seven deadly sins. Envy requires a lot of money. Enough money to be Free is all I ever needed.

BIBLIOGRAPHY

ALAN LAKEIN, *How To Get Control of Your Time and Life* (New York: Peter H. Wyden, Inc.,1973)

Bruce H. Mann, *Republic of Debtors: Bankruptcy in the Age of American Independence* (Cambridge, Harvard University Press, 2002)

David Wagner, *The Poorhouse America's Forgotten Institution,* (Laham,MD, Rowan & Littlefield Publishers, Inc., 2005)